The Good Enough Manager

D0023860

The premise of this title is that it is rare, if indeed impossible, to find "perfect" managers that are viewed as such by all those that serve under them. Therefore it is better to strive to become a good enough manager, leading and meeting the needs of all. The movement to strive for excellence is fine but hard to put into practice for all personality types, thus the goal is to be the best we can possibly be without the pressure of achieving the unachievable.

Aaron J. Nurick is Professor of Management and Psychology at Bentley University. Dr. Nurick's teaching and scholarship have been devoted to the application of psychology to management and organizations. His published work includes articles in the *Academy of Management Learning and Education Journal, Journal of Management Inquiry, Psychological Bulletin, Human Relations, Human Resource Management, Organizational Behavior Teaching Review, Journal of Management Education, Business Horizons,* and *Human Resource Planning.*

The Good Enough Manager
The Making of a GEM

AARON J. NURICK, Ph.D.

Routledge
Taylor & Francis Group

NEW YORK AND LONDON

First published 2012
by Routledge
711 Third Avenue, New York, NY 10017

Simultaneously published in the UK
by Routledge
2 Park Square, Milton Park, Abingdon, Oxon OX14 4RN

Routledge is an imprint of the Taylor & Francis Group, an informa business

Library of Congress Cataloging-in-Publication Data
Nurick, Aaron J.
  The good enough manager : the making of a gem / Aaron Nurick.
  p. cm.
  Includes index.
  1. Management. 2. Executive ability. 3. Leadership. I. Title.
  HD31.N857 2011
  658.4'09–dc23

                                                            2011017362

ISBN: 978-0-415-88533-1 (hbk)
ISBN: 978-0-415-88534-8 (pbk)
ISBN: 978-0-203-35733-0 (ebk)

Typeset in Garamond
by Wearset Ltd, Boldon, Tyne and Wear

Printed and bound in the United States of America on acid-free paper
by Walsworth Publishing Company, Marceline, MO.

SUSTAINABLE
FORESTRY
INITIATIVE

Certified Sourcing
www.sfiprogram.org
SFI-00555
The SFI label applies to the text stock.

To my students, past and present...

Contents

Preface

There is something about turning the watershed age of 60 that leads one to examine the arc of his life and career, and search for connecting threads of meaning. I published my first book over 25 years ago. It was an outgrowth of my doctoral dissertation and the culmination of a research project that formed the first stage of my professional life. It combined extensive survey research, and quantitative and qualitative analysis supported by the extensive resources of my graduate program at the University of Tennessee. I was also fortunate at the time to work with colleagues at the Institute for Social Research at the University of Michigan who were kind enough to hire me as a graduate research assistant for their quality of work life field research project at the Tennessee Valley Authority. This second volume brings together many varied ideas and pursuits that have informed my thinking, teaching and scholarship since the mid 1980s: interpersonal relations in management (the title of my major course); emotional intelligence and psychoanalytic theory applied to organizations; art and music; and personal history. Together these two works form the literal bookends of this 25-year span.

This book is both a scholarly and a personal work. The central idea of the "good enough manager" has been with me for a long time. I was introduced to the ideas of D.W. Winnicott, and his conceptualization of the "good enough mother," when I sought to broaden and deepen my knowledge of organizational psychology to include psychoanalytic theory. As I became fascinated by the ideas of such thinkers as Abraham Zaleznik, Manfred Kets de Vries, and Harry Levinson, who were applying the principles of Freudian and object relations theories to organizational life and leadership, I started down a path that diverged from my graduate training in organizational psychology and teaching of organizational behavior in my early years at Bentley University.

Since he was located nearby at Harvard, I sought the wise counsel of Abe Zaleznik and he encouraged me to seek formal clinical training, which I pursued first through an extension course on psychoanalytic theory at the Boston Psychoanalytic Society and Institute, and then as an "extern" in training for two years at the Boston Institute for Psychotherapy. It was there, under the guidance of wonderful teachers and challenging supervisors, that I began to put these ideas into practice while working with clients. Although I never developed a private practice as a psychotherapist, and remained a full-time academic, the training and experience have informed my teaching, writing, and consulting for over two decades. Harry Levinson sponsored my membership in the International Society for the Psychoanalytic Study of Organizations, and has been a cherished friend and mentor to this day. ISPSO has been for me a major source of intellectual stimulation, from colleagues from all over the world who take a deeper look at organizational life.

While the conceptual framework had been percolating and evolving for a long time, I finally began to sketch the beginnings of this book while I was co-teaching a course at Xiamen University in China. I took advantage of the uncertainty and dislocation I was feeling, heightened by a combination of much unstructured time, very limited Internet access, and a dearth of English-speaking colleagues, print materials, and television beyond *National Geographic* and *Biz China*. I used that reflective space – a major theme in this book – and the idea of a GEM came into being. I then needed real-life data to illustrate the theory. With the kind assistance of very helpful colleagues at Bentley University, I was able to reach out to a large population of business professionals and the study described in Chapter 2 came to fruition during the following year.

This book is intended for multiple audiences, perhaps most especially practicing managers, but also including teachers, researchers, and students in the fields of management and organizational behavior and psychology. To that end, the book is written from a rather personal perspective, very much in line with the way I teach about these issues in the classroom and in executive seminars. I include personal reflections about my own experiences and history in relation to the data and ideas presented. I make connections between management, psychology, the arts and music, as well as historical and current business, cultural, and societal trends.

The first chapter provides the background and theoretical overview of the idea of a "good enough manager" (or GEM). The research study is presented in Chapter 2 with a focus more on the applied nature of the findings. Chapters 3–5 illuminate the major findings of the study, with the descriptions and narratives about managers provided by the survey respondents. I have preserved the actual words of respondents in the selected excerpts with only minor edits for spelling, grammar, clarification, and preservation of confidentiality. In Chapter 6 I provide lessons and challenge the reader to think about how to put these concepts into practice, with a strong emphasis on developing a deeper emotional capacity or mindset. Although I am prescriptive, I try to avoid simple "how to" lists that would be more appropriate for a text or workbook. I conclude each section with "Lessons for GEMs" that summarize the formulations and prescriptions that come before.

It is probably evident from this description and history that this book, like so many other works, represents the synthesis of many schools of thought, and derives its definition through important professional and personal relationships I have experienced with individuals too numerous to acknowledge herein. I do, however, wish to express my gratitude to those who most directly assisted with the research I undertook, and enhanced the preparation and writing of this manuscript. First and foremost, I wish to thank the 1,058 anonymous respondents to my web survey. Their ideas and stories about the "best" and "worst" managers in their professional experience gave life and confirmation to many of the theoretical ideas. The selected excerpts are the proverbial "tip of the iceberg" as they represent many others who expressed similar ideas and experiences. Kim Bridgeo (former Director), and other colleagues in the Bentley University Office of Institutional Research, along with Dee Lane in the Office of University Advancement, assisted me in setting up and disseminating the survey, creating a secure database, and organizing the responses into an accessible and useful form. Bayar Tumennasan and Maria Skaletsky in the Bentley University Academic Technology Center were extremely patient and helpful as they guided me through the science and art of SPSS Textual Analysis.

Beyond Winnicott, I have been inspired by the deep knowledge and wisdom of several very influential scholars, most notably: Harry Levinson, Abe Zaleznik, Manfred Kets de Vries, the late Larry Gould, Ed Shapiro, Howard Gardner, Daniel Goleman, Steven Stein, Howard Book, Howard Stein, Michael Diamond, Peter Salovey, David Caruso, Rueven Bar-On, Peter Vaill, Elliot Aronson, the late Anne Alonso, Scott Rutan, Cecil Rice, Robert French, Jim Krantz, Larry Hirshhorn, Lionel Stapley, Stanley Gold, Ken Eisold, Susan Long, and Gordon Lawrence. All of these individuals (along with many others) interweave organizational and social psychology, management theory, practice and consulting, psychoanalysis, emotional intelligence, and psychotherapy, and their ideas and words grace the pages you are about to read.

I am grateful to Routledge, especially Business Editor John Szilagyi, who saw promise in my original GEM idea and proposal and consistently encouraged and supported me throughout the production of this book. I appreciate the helpful comments of the many anonymous reviewers of the proposal and draft chapters that helped to sharpen the focus and clarify the presentation of my ideas.

On a more personal level, I am the beneficiary of many "good enough facilitating environments," from my parents and the family store of my upbringing, through various institutions of higher learning, a university setting for my career, and many close and loving relationships. Several close friends and colleagues contributed to my thinking and supported my work: Tony Buono, Judy Kamm, Greg Hall, George Sousa, Joe Weiss, Carole Thomas, David Fedo, Moira Ounjian, and Vicki LaFarge. My wife, Diane Austin, my loving partner in life for over 30 years, carefully and with a keen and discerning eye, read original drafts and greatly contributed to my thinking and writing, just as she enriches my life in countless other ways.

A major theme running throughout the study and this book is teaching. I have dedicated my professional life to teaching and learning in multiple roles, and I dedicate this work to the thousands of students who have populated my classroom and brought joy and meaning to my life.

one

Introduction

What is a "Good Enough" Manager?

The perfect is the enemy of the good.

—Voltaire

Humans are complex social and emotional beings. Relationships forged in the earliest stages of our existence are continually recast and recreated as we bring these interpersonal elements of our humanity into new relationships in all realms of life, including the workplace. This book is based on a primary principle: *just as there is no such thing as a perfect parent, managing people in organizations is an inherently human and fallible endeavor, mainly because managing occurs by and through human relationships.* The central questions addressed in the following chapters are: how do the "best" managers behave? What sets them apart from their peers? What impact do they have on their subordinates and co-workers? What can we learn from them?

Whenever I am introduced to someone and reveal my identity as an organizational psychologist and management professor, the response is often a variation of "You need to come to my company," or "My boss is nuts." As a culture, we hold ambivalent views about those who supervise and manage our workplaces. While we long for strong leaders who take charge and solve problems, we sometimes resist when a leader actually puts his or her authority into practice. Maybe it is a built-in suspicion and skepticism of authority or our simultaneous admiration, fear, envy, and contempt directed at those whom we elevate to positions of status and power. Often "the boss" is the subject of ridicule and the butt of jokes in the form of characters and caricatures on television and in other media, such as the comic sections of newspapers. This ambivalence is brilliantly depicted in the somewhat lovable yet dangerously incompetent character of Michael Scott in the popular television comedy *The Office*. The newspaper comics are less subtle, as managers are shown to be amoral and clueless buffoons like Dilbert's pointy-haired and nameless boss, or explosive, hostile tyrants such as the aptly-named Mr. Dithers, the tormentor of Blondie's husband, Dagwood Bumstead.

While most corporate leaders quietly manage their companies out of the limelight, a chosen few of today's CEOs have blended into our celebrity culture. Individuals like Bill Gates, Steve Jobs, Jack Welch, and Richard Branson are innovators and leaders who have become larger-than-life media figures accorded the celebrity status we give to rock stars, athletes, and politicians; and they are our modern-day barons similar to Rockefeller, Morgan, and Carnegie who dominated the business world a century ago. Others such as Donald Trump and Martha Stewart have transcended their corporate roles and are famous (or infamous) media personas with mega-brands, and exist at the center of multiple media shaped in their image. While we may enjoy reading their books, and watching their television, news, tabloid (and court) appearances, the mega-bosses, who may have a profound effect on business innovation, culture, and modern life (think iPad and *The Apprentice*), are not necessarily the ones who have the most immediate impact on the work life of the typical employee. Most of us interact with day-to-day managers who try to anticipate and respond to a multitude of economic, social, and behavioral challenges in order to accomplish the goals of a company or other organization.

Business observers say that bosses get too much credit or blame for the performance of their companies, in keeping with the human tendency to attribute success or failure to the person and downplay the complex interplay of systems, markets, and external forces beyond the leader's control. Yet, research on managerial behavior reinforces the fact that immediate supervisors can have a profound effect on their employees and co-workers, even to the point of influencing their mental and physical health. One study demonstrated that a bad boss can dramatically increase the incidence of employee heart attacks by as much as 20 to 40 percent.[1] The behavior of the manager permeates and shapes the culture of an organization. Employees at lower levels keenly observe and even mimic their managers' actions, as organizations function in a similar manner as the status hierarchies of primates and other animals. Neurotic bosses create "neurotic organizations" as employees act out the paranoid, compulsive, dramatic, or inhibited behavior of the leaders.[2] Given the immediate impact of bosses on the well-being of their employees, it is no wonder that managers are the focus of a multi-billion dollar consulting industry aimed at promoting, training, and coaching them, evidenced by a plethora of motivational and inspirational programs and books providing *six sigmas* or *seven habits* in our never-ending *search for excellence* – and wanting to accomplish it all in *one minute*.

My continuing interest in the behavior of managers comes from nearly 40 years of observing, studying, teaching, and writing about those who try their best to organize and lead groups and organizations. Fueled originally by youthful idealism and the perpetual curiosity of a graduate student, my life's work has been about finding ways to improve work life and to make workplaces more human and humane. Most of my efforts have been in the classroom, teaching the psychological underpinnings of life in organizations to undergraduate and graduate students, with an occasional foray into management training and organizational consulting along the same themes. Rather than taking the strategic perspective of "the view at 30,000 feet," my focus is more at the micro-level – the daily interactions and relationships that shape and color one's immediate work experience and its emotional undercurrents.

The fields of management and organizational behavior are replete with theories and practical guides to leadership, dating back to early management scholars such as Chester Barnard and the prolific writings of Peter Drucker.[3] My own "interpersonal relations" view has been historically shaped more by the ideas of the organizational humanists: Elton Mayo, Fritz Roethlisberger, Douglas McGregor, Kurt Lewin, Eric Trist, and their intellectual descendants: Abraham Zaleznik, Harry Levinson, Chris Argyris, Warren Bennis, Manfred Kets de Vries, Anthony Athos, and John Gabarro. As described by Roethlisberger in his autobiography, these scholars, who came to prominence in the 1950s and 1960s, were greatly influenced by the clinical, humanistic, and existential psychologists of the era such as Carl Rogers, Abraham Maslow, Erich Fromm, and James Bugental.[4] Their emphasis was on the social system, group dynamics, and interpersonal processes and took institutional form at the Harvard Business School, MIT, the University of Michigan Center for Group Dynamics, the Tavistock Institute of Human Relations in London, and the National Training Laboratories in Washington, D.C. and Bethel, Maine. My doctoral research was a direct outgrowth of this intellectual tradition. In my dissertation, I concluded that more direct employee participation in organizational change processes increased their ownership and acceptance of changes, and satisfaction with their work life. This work was firmly grounded in the cognitive-empirical (and highly statistical) domain of my graduate training in organizational psychology. The focus was on showing relationships among measured variables, such as the degree of employee participation and perceived influence (measured on five-point scales) and determining the significance of the results. While the outcomes were illuminating and useful, important questions remained: how do managers create such environments? What attitudes and skills are necessary, and how are these developed?

As my thinking deepened, I diverged from the cognitive and linear models and became more fascinated with psychodynamic interpretations of organizational life, largely influenced by my own experience and training in psychotherapy, and my study and many years of teaching of interpersonal relations in management. It is at this deeper level that one can reveal something beyond surface behavior and begin to approach what is the essence or perhaps something that approaches the soul of a human being. As the writer David Brooks describes, it is "the unconscious realm of emotions, intuitions, biases, longings, genetic predispositions, character traits, and social norms" that guides our behavior, decisions, and relationships.[5] Building upon my appreciation for and understanding of these unconscious processes, I embraced the "object relations" theories that specifically focus on those significant relationships created in the earliest stages of human development, and that continue to be recreated in various forms throughout one's life. My study and inquiry led to the discovery of a compelling underlying idea: *good enough*.

The Meaning of *Good Enough*

The concept of "good enough" is based on the psychological theories of Donald Winnicott, a British pediatrician and psychoanalyst who observed and developed ideas about humans' earliest interpersonal encounters. His approach to his clinical work with children and patients has been described as deeply personal and intuitive, and he came into each encounter as an authentic presence, feeling the mutual interactions "in one's bones," maintaining a paradoxical balance between discipline and freedom.[6] Such an intuitive orientation begins in our earliest relationships. In Winnicott's view the "good enough" mother provides an atmosphere known as a "holding environment" where an infant learns to develop a sense of himself as an autonomous and genuine self in relation to the mother (now, of course, including the father, or other primary caretakers). Through early interactions that are primarily nonverbal, the mother allows her child to react to her inevitable imperfections, natural absences, and other "failures." As Winnicott states: "The good-enough mother ... starts off with an almost complete adaptation to her infant's needs, and as time proceeds she adapts less and less completely, gradually, according to the infant's growing ability to deal with her failure".[7] This primary relationship is presented as a process of continuous mutual adaptation, a balance between the mother's complete control and the child's developing independence, ultimately creating the foundation for the experience and development of *interdependence* in relationships. The balancing of these forces requires one to work at the boundary between certainty and uncertainty, and the known and the unknown that provides the basis for continued learning and growth.[8] The *good enough mother* has the capacity to observe and question her own actions and potential shortcomings, and to respond with empathy to the needs and emotional reactions of her growing child. She can suspend her certainty about what is happening in the child's developing inner world and remain open and responsive to his experiences, including his struggles and expressed frustrations with her inevitable "failures."[9]

As this mutual process evolves and elaborates over time, this good enough mother recognizes that ultimately she cannot (and should not) be all and do all. By acknowledging her limitations, she sends an implicit message that her child is a separate and unique person *in relation to her*, and can claim a measure of personal freedom and ownership of his internal world which he may in turn choose to share with others.[10] By contrast, a parent who, out of anxiety and insecurity, tries too hard to control every aspect of the child's life (or, in a word, tries to be perfect) has the opposite effect. This rigid certainty is met by the child's formation of a defensive shell, or "false self" that "behaves as if he were the child the parent needs, rather than the child he is."[11] By trying to manage and serve the parent's needs, the child hides his true and genuine self, stifling meaningful interactions and creativity. One can observe this in today's hovering "helicopter" parents, as well intentioned as they are, striving to control and manage so many aspects of their children's lives well into early adulthood. Educators observe that, although many of these children are high achievers and results-driven, they are not as good at finding their own way through complex systems or coping with unplanned or unintended circumstances. Given a "good enough" environment, however, a growing child learns to navigate the complexities and imperfections of genuine human relationships, as this primary relationship forms a template for future relationships, including those in organizations and the larger culture.

Granted, managers are not parents and employees are not children; however, as authority figures, leaders and managers carry the residue of our earliest authority relationships and the vestiges of these interpersonal encounters are continually re-visited in new settings. In a recent *Harvard Business Review* blog posting, management consultant Peter Bregman came to a similar conclusion upon observing the interaction between a mother and her child in New York's Central Park. He lists several aspects that link parenting with managing: expressing care, practicing patience, leveraging uniqueness, developing independent capability, and setting appropriate expectations and boundaries.[12] In transposing ideas about good enough parenting to "good enough managing" in organizations, several important themes and implications begin to emerge.

Good Enough Means Letting Go of Perfection

American business, and perhaps western culture in general, is infatuated with winning, and striving for and attaining, excellence and perfection. It is now said that the American Dream is no longer about seizing the opportunity to attain aspirations through hard work; it is about transcending those aspirations and realizing perfection.[13] From childhood on we receive implicit and explicit messages about achieving excellence, often expressed as rankings and awards for the top schools, neighborhoods, celebrities, restaurants, and CEOs. Much has been written about the stress of over-managed children who begin prepping for top colleges while still in pre-school, while neglecting the importance and value of unstructured play. The media bombard us with visions of the perfect family, gift, holiday, job, or body, and provide ready formulas for how to attain these, usually attached to the selling of a book or product. The emphasis is often focused more on the celebration of the outcome rather than the process and journey of discovery and learning along the way. The downside is that we are often set up for failure, since achieving these expectations of perfection is rarely possible, leading to even higher rates of stress, anxiety, depression, and varieties of interpersonal dysfunction.

There is nothing wrong with setting high goals and striving for them through excellent performance. In fact, motivation theories have long stressed the importance of goal setting and working toward challenging yet achievable accomplishments.[14] When caught up in our perfectionist struggle, however, we sometimes forget that we can also find beauty in imperfection. Japanese culture has a term for this concept known as *wabi-sabi* that forms an entire aesthetic of Zen simplicity and the appreciation of nature as imperfect, impermanent, and incomplete. Such an orientation to work is more often the province of artists, designers, philosophers, and poets as their focus is more on the process of making or creating rather than the achievement of the final product.[15]

The writer Michael Pollan invoked this line of thought in his book *A Place of My Own*, in which he carefully documents his efforts to design and build a one-room writing structure:

> I took heart in what I'd read about the Arts and Crafts movement's liberal line on mistakes: "There is hope in honest error," one designer had declared, "none in the icy perfections of the mere stylist." Small mistakes in the finished product revealed the hand of the worker; perfection was opaque.[16]

The same phenomenon of natural imperfection as part of the creative process occurs in other art forms such as music, dance, and theater. Yo-Yo Ma is perhaps our greatest living cellist, often referred to as a rock star of classical music, drawing huge and enthusiastic crowds to concert venues. At his level of talent and expertise, we might presume that he would be fixated on accurately playing all the notes the composer set out in the score. Yet, when he was interviewed about his early years as a musician, he described the following scenario:

> I've tried to play a "perfect" concert.... I had worked my butt off, practicing four hours a day – a lot for me – and knew the music inside out. While sitting there at the concert, playing all the notes correctly, I started to wonder, "Why am I here? I'm doing everything as planned. So, what's at stake? Nothing. Not only is the audience bored but I myself am bored." Perfection is not very communicative. However, when you subordinate your technique to the musical message you get really involved. Then you can take risks. It doesn't matter if you fail. What does matter is that you tried.[17]

That spirit of adventure has enabled Yo-Yo Ma to experiment with new musical and artistic forms, such as his Silk Road Project, a highly collaborative, global, artistic and educational enterprise that links ancient traditions and cultures with modern art forms.[18] It is the same innovative spirit that animates the improvisation found in modern jazz as musicians bend the notes and rhythms and "play" within the defined harmonic structure. They also listen carefully and mutually adapt to each other's playing as the music unfolds in unpredictable patterns. The jazz pianist Herbie Hancock told the story of his early experience playing with the Miles Davis band and clearly (and embarrassingly) hitting the wrong note. Instead of stopping and admonishing the young musician, Davis simply shifted on the fly, adapted the music to the mistake, and created something totally new, along with the enduring admiration of his newest band member.[19]

One can translate the idea of imperfection and suspending certainty to drama and the theater as seen in this commentary about the contemporary actress Cate Blanchett:

> In work and life, Blanchett, whose favorite word is "fluidity," has a kind of inconclusiveness that lets her remain receptive. "I don't like everything to be tied neatly in bows," she told me. "If it's flowing, you don't arrest it." Keeping things open when you're acting, she explained, reinforces the mystery and the intensity of the moment.[20]

Or, consider the work of choreographer Twyla Tharp, as she documents her creative process:

> This, to me, is the most interesting paradox of creativity: In order to be habitually creative, you have to know how to prepare to be creative, but good planning alone won't make your efforts successful; it's only after you let go of your plans that you can breathe life into your efforts.[21]

In each of these reflections on their artistic endeavors, the artists bring technical competence and mastery – even brilliance – to their ventures, however, for each performer certainty and perfection are not the main points of their creation. The paradox is that they achieve artistic excellence by *letting go* of predetermined ideas and patterns, and allowing room for something unique to emerge.

At this point it is important to pause and make a clear and important distinction: it is tempting in our culture of idealistic perfection to believe that "good enough" is tantamount to mediocrity, getting by, or settling for something that is average or adequate. We often hear bromides such as "good enough never is" or "good enough for government work."[22] This limited view simply is not the case here and Winnicott's metaphor has a much deeper and more complex meaning. A *good enough* environment, as earlier described, can actually provide a pathway to more creative and innovative actions, and ultimately lead to even better performance. Good enough *managing* (the process) is not the same as good enough *performance* (the outcome). In this view, one does not let go of the quest for excellence; rather it is more the letting go of the *perfectionist behavior* that can ultimately impede the way to better performance. In order to continuously improve, one must embrace and learn from mistakes. We can see this tension between orderly and predictive innovation and the messier and discontinuous creative process playing out at companies such as 3M. When efficiency and cost-reducing techniques of a Six Sigma measurement culture are applied to a creative process, new ideas that don't fit known, desired (and therefore presumed correct) outcomes can be stifled, and that can prove limiting in an economy that is oriented more to the percolation of ideas and designs that no one ever thought of before.[23]

Recent research on cognitive functioning concludes that, although human beings hate to be wrong and are often shamed by errors, it is our capacity to make mistakes and learn from them that can be viewed as strength. Kathryn Schultz states it this way:

> As ashamed as we may feel of our mistakes, they are not a byproduct of all that's worst about being human. On the contrary: They're a byproduct of all that's best about us. We don't get things wrong because we are uninformed and lazy and stupid and evil. We get things wrong because we get things right. The more scientists understand about cognitive functioning, the more it becomes clear that our capacity to err is utterly inextricable from what makes the human brain so swift, adaptable, and intelligent.[24]

Of course, errors can be costly. Sometimes it really *is* rocket science or brain surgery. Our tendency to resist and cover up mistakes actually creates cultures unwilling to do anything about them. As an example of learning from mistakes, both the aviation and health care industries have developed systems and cultures that encourage the open reporting of errors to help ensure that they won't happen again. Also, several states have introduced "I'm sorry" laws that prevent physicians' apologies for errors to be used against them in malpractice suits. As Schultz concludes:

> If it behooves companies in such material and moral ways to accept their fallibility and own up to their mistakes, surely the same goes for each of us as individuals – and for all of us as a community. Recognizing that error is an inevitable part of our lives frees us from despising ourselves – and forbids us from looking down on others – for getting things wrong.... We can respond to the mistakes (or putative mistakes) of those around us with empathy and generosity.[25]

A "good enough" environment that embraces fallibility is established by a manager who suspends certainty, and incorporates the unknown and uncertain by interpreting, adapting, and improvising in the moment. Imperfection is built into the creative process. As a prime example of this philosophy, leadership expert Charlene Li describes how Domino's Pizza openly admitted in their advertising that they had determined that their product was in need of improvement. They made changes and invited the public to try the newly improved product. As a result they were celebrated for their openness and "bold and refreshing" candor, and sales and profits rose.[26] Based on this experience, Li concludes that managers need to create cultures where failure is admitted, risk is rewarded, and rules of engagement for managing failures clearly defined.

Creating these cultures requires a new mindset. The writer and cultural observer Daniel Pink claims that "right brain" aptitudes that are more simultaneous, metaphorical, aesthetic, contextual, and synthetic, will greatly determine who succeeds the future.[27] He echoes others who suggest that those who are more creative, empathic, and conceptual thinkers, in comparison to logical left brain thinkers more traditionally associated with business and management, are more adaptive to what he calls the Conceptual Age. He describes six "senses," uniting the left and right brain hemispheres, like two sections of an orchestra:

1   Not just function, but also **design** – creating something beautiful, whimsical, and emotionally engaging.
2   Not just argument, but also **story-telling** – shaping and communicating a compelling narrative.
3   Not just focus, but also **symphony** – synthesizing information, seeing the larger picture, crossing boundaries, and combining the parts into a meaningful whole.

4   Not just logic, but also **empathy** – understanding others, building relationships and caring for others.
5   Not just seriousness, but also **play** – injecting laughter, humor and games into work and life.
6   Not just accumulation, but also **meaning** – finding a higher purpose that creates transcendence.[28]

The essential components of this conceptual orientation are very consistent with Winnicott's "good enough" human development process that emphasizes the importance of empathy, play, and the mutual creation of meaning in the primary mother–child relationship. The capacity to reflect on experience and suspend certainty is central to the development of these important early relationships. In a famous letter to his brothers about his artistic desires, the eighteenth-century poet John Keats referred to this reflective capacity as *negative capability*, or the ability to be in "uncertainties, mysteries, doubts, without any irritable reaching after fact and reason."[29] From our earliest interactions we learn that human relationships are uncertain and ultimately imperfect. The writer Anne Morrow Lindbergh elegantly captured many of these interpersonal themes in her landmark book *Gift from the Sea*. In her meditation about our closest relationships she observes:

> We insist on permanency, on duration, on continuity; when the only continuity possible, in life as in love, is in growth, in fluidity – in freedom, in the sense that the dancers are free, barely touching as they pass, but partners in the same pattern.[30]

Just as her dancers experience freedom and autonomy within the bounds of a relationship, successful managers accept and even embrace fluidity and uncertainty as a way of life within organizational structures. They can also recognize and accept their own limitations and imperfections and relate to their roles, tasks, and colleagues with acceptance and a measure of humility.

Good Enough is About Emotional Intelligence

Good enough managing means being able to appreciate, tolerate, and navigate a complex emotional terrain. Managers set the emotional tone in an organization, and employees look to their leaders to define expectations and to be responsive to their concerns. There is an enduring fantasy that emotions have no place in business. This line of reasoning is a holdover from the mechanistic ideal of "scientific management" that was the model of business during the industrial age in the early twentieth century, and that still influences much of modern management thought.[31] The emphasis is on precise measurement, logical thinking, rational decisions, and mechanical certainty.

Cognitive supremacy triumphs over emotional experience and emotional expression is seen as unprofessional, an unnecessary distraction, or even worse, a human failure. This line of reasoning tends to confuse the experience of emotions with how the emotions are displayed and discharged.

Our current digital age is marked by forces that dramatically impinge on the emotional functioning of human beings. Communication is constant, instant, and ubiquitous. Alvin Toffler's world of "future shock," so compellingly predicted in the late 1960s at the dawn of the information age, has come roaring into the twenty-first century as change occurs at an ever increasing pace.[32] As much as we multi-task, check email in the middle of the night, update our Facebook profiles, and cannot conceive of life without being constantly connected, it is hard to keep up and the stress takes its toll. Peter Vaill captured this phenomenon 20 years ago with his metaphor of "permanent whitewater" as managers struggle to navigate treacherous currents in the turbulent business environment that has only increased during the recent economic crisis.[33]

It is not surprising that the concept of *emotional intelligence* has captured the imagination of business professionals and consultants in the last several years. Howard Gardner's idea of multiple intelligences, defining a wider range of abilities such as the kinesthetic, mathematical, and linguistic, expanded our concept of human capacity that was usually limited to the cognitive domain, or what is commonly referred to as IQ. Gardner also introduced the idea of *personal* intelligences that draw upon one's ability to work with people in social environments.[34] Several researchers have explored this more complex view of ability in the form of emotional intelligence or EQ, defined by Reuven Bar-On as: "An array of non-cognitive personal, emotional, and social capabilities, competencies and skills that influence one's ability to succeed in coping with environmental demands and pressures."[35] The interest in emotional intelligence exploded with the publication of Daniel Goleman's bestselling book, *Emotional Intelligence*, which introduced the idea to a much broader audience, most notably business leaders and organizational consultants.[36] Since then numerous articles, books, measurement instruments, and training programs have served to turn the idea into a commodity that promises to transform organizations. Although there is ongoing debate about precise definitions of emotional intelligence[37] and dangers of over-dramatizing the impact of an idea that has intuitive appeal and scholarly validity, several aspects are very relevant to the "good enough" approach:

- Emotions are an essential part of our biological make-up and cannot be set aside or turned off like a light switch. In fact, as Goleman documents, emotions are an inextricable part of decision-making, as evidenced by those people, who for organic reasons have limited access to their emotional centers in the brain, struggle to make even the simplest decisions.[38]

- Definitions of emotional intelligence focus on both *intra-personal* (self awareness) and *interpersonal* (empathy and relationship) dimensions. These twin capacities form the basis of the ability to simultaneously reflect and connect.
- Unlike cognitive intelligence (or IQ) that is relatively fixed, emotional intelligence can be improved with education and practice. Although many of the abilities associated with emotional intelligence, such as empathy and emotional self-awareness, are developed early in life and emerge over time, other specific skills such as assertive communication and active listening can be improved with appropriate training and coaching.

Good Enough is About Facilitating, Responding, and Adapting

The "good enough" concept is consistent with the historical evolution of ideas about leading and managing. Leadership theory and research have followed a progression from emphasizing

1   the *traits* of the leader, including such individual characteristics as self-confidence, emotional intelligence and integrity;
2   the *behavior* of the leader in role, such as whether the leader is more autocratic or democratic in their style; and
3   the interaction of the style of the leader with the organizational situation, or how leaders change their style under different circumstances or *contingencies*.[39]

   Much of the early research on organizational leadership focused on a choice between seemingly polar opposites, such as whether the leader placed more emphasis on the task or on relationships, or viewed their employees as inherently disliking work and in need of control, or as naturally creative and productive if given enough freedom to do their work. Douglas McGregor's presentation of Theory X and Theory Y, perhaps the cornerstone of managerial assumptions about human nature, lives on to this day.[40] Theory X fits the scientific management mindset that workers need to be controlled and externally motivated while Theory Y assumes that under the right circumstances, workers can be more intrinsically motivated and exercise more autonomy. Even in current organizational life, one hears mention of the "carrot or the stick" that Harry Levinson once critiqued as the "great jackass fallacy," noting that human beings are much more complex than the animal referenced in such simplistic and reductive motivational techniques. Levinson instead focuses on movement toward the *ego ideal*, the image that individuals carry of themselves at their future best. Like Maslow's concept of self-actualization, the ego ideal is the distant goal, the peak of perfection to which one aspires but never fully reaches. The alignment, however, between the perceptions of one's present state (the self-image) and the ego ideal affects self-esteem and overall well-being. The closer the alignment, the better we feel.[41]

Contemporary thinkers see leading and managing as a more fluid and adaptive process in relation to employees, more in keeping with the contingency approach. Ken Blanchard's "situational leadership model" presents the four leadership styles of directing, coaching, supporting, and delegating. The leader adapts his or her style depending on the level of development or "maturity" of the employee.[42] In somewhat similar fashion, Ronald Heifetz depicts the leader identifying and presenting an adaptive challenge and then, using a pressure cooker analogy, adjusting the heat to the level where employees are able to tolerate it without "blowing the vessel."[43] To Heifetz, formal and informal authority helps to form the holding environment as the "containing vessel" for the stresses of change.

In many ways, the good enough approach described earlier provides the psychological foundation that enables a manager to adapt to continually changing circumstances. The idea of "containing" strong emotions is central to managing with emotional intelligence, and reinforces the facilitating or holding environment and the structure of tasks, roles, and boundaries that leads to increased trust, growth, and perspective.[44] The manner in which managers navigate complex relationships can make the difference between a work experience that fosters effective performance, innovation, growth, and development, and one that stifles or stands in the way of employee potential.

Leader, Manager ... or Both?

Throughout these discussions there is a pervasive question about the similarities and differences between managing and leading as the two terms are used interchangeably. Can a manager be a leader and vice versa? Leadership scholar and psychoanalyst Abraham Zaleznik sees clear differences, concluding that managers and leaders have different psychological orientations. Managers are more likely to seek and maintain order and control while leaders are more tolerant of chaos, lack of structure, and uncertainty. Leaders are more like artists, scientists, and other creative thinkers.[45] John Kotter also sees differences, but focuses on the idea that they represent two distinct yet complementary systems of action, both are necessary, and leadership is neither superior to nor a replacement for management. Management is about coping with complexity and bringing order to often chaotic circumstances by functions such as planning and budgeting, organizing and staffing, and controlling and problem solving. Leadership is more about coping with change brought about by the increasingly volatile business environment through setting a direction or vision, aligning people by communicating the new direction, and motivating and inspiring, appealing more to needs, values, and emotions. In Kotter's view, strong leadership with weak management is often worse than the reverse and the challenge is to find the balance. Successful companies can learn the differences and seek to develop leader-managers.[46]

Finally, a more integrative view is provided by Jonathan Gosling and Henry Mintzberg. As they warn:

> Nobody aspires to be a good manager anymore; everybody wants to be a great leader. But the separation of management from leadership is dangerous. Just as management without leadership encourages an uninspired style, which deadens activities, leadership without management encourages a disconnected style, which promotes hubris.[47]

In their management development program, they emphasize the balance between action and reflection, encompassing five "mindsets" or ways that managers interpret and deal with what is going on around them:

1 managing self – the reflective mindset
2 managing organizations – the analytic mindset
3 managing context – the worldly mindset
4 managing relationships – the collaborative mindset
5 managing change – the action mindset.

These mindsets overlap and Gosling and Mintzberg use the metaphor of the manager weaving each under and over the other to create a fine, sturdy and coherent cloth that can be combined with others, creating seams that are finely sewn. This fabric that combines simultaneous awareness of the self, the other, the relationship, and behavior in the changing context provides the containing and facilitating "good enough" environment as the foundation for all kinds of relationships.

Definition of a Good Enough Manager

A theme running throughout this book is the continuous dance between the human impulses of control and freedom, the known and unknown, and finding a point of equilibrium or balance. Rather than being seen as opposing forces, they interact in patterns in human relationships, each defining the other, and the point of balance is a moving target achieved by constant interaction, trial and error, and emotional attunement. The stage is now set to explore the idea of a *good enough manager* in greater depth. From this overview, the following definition will serve as our starting point. A *good enough* manager:

- is confident working with fluidity, complexity and uncertainty;
- builds and maintains effective relationships by managing emotions and communicating clearly and genuinely (and encouraging the same in others);
- facilitates autonomy, maturity, creativity, and growth.

The following chapters are devoted to discovering and exploring good enough managers whom I refer to by the fortuitous acronym GEMs, because they are highly valued and precious. The ideas and conclusions are based on a comprehensive study of employee observations about their "best" and "worst" managers and using these descriptions and stories to illustrate the behavior of GEMs in action. The narratives, presented as selected excerpts in the words of the 1,000 plus study respondents, provide an intriguing glimpse into the lives of day-to-day employees and their managers, highlighting the best and worst practices from a very human (and sometimes humorous) perspective, and illustrating the central "good enough" premise. The vignettes include stories of unsung heroes and small-minded tyrants, but mostly portray very human characters that go to work each day and find a way to bring out the best in their employees. These are the managers we want to work for and hate to leave. They are adaptive to our current turbulent work environment and the needs of both the organization and their employees. They are the ones who release creative thinking, and motivate and inspire great performance. They do it by *facilitating* rather than commanding or controlling, and by negotiating the precarious equilibrium between holding on and letting go.

two

Discovering GEMs

A Study of the Best and Worst Managers

It was the best of times, it was the worst of times....

–Charles Dickens

Having now provided a theoretical basis and a working definition of a *good enough manager*, it is important to see how the idea reveals itself in practice. In an effort to discover the underlying themes of the behavior of a good enough manager, the following research study documents an exploration of how managers function in their roles from the standpoint of their employees.

Approach and Data Collection

There is a segment in my Interpersonal Relations in Management course when I ask students to recall the "best" and "worst" bosses or managers with whom they have worked and identify significant aspects of their behavior. After they record their individual observations, I then open the discussion to the entire class and note common themes. Each semester, variations on similar basic themes for the "best" managers emerge: trust, honesty, support, encouragement, listening, and respect. More experienced graduate students often add comments such as "encourages me to take risks" or "allows me to fail," highlighting a willingness of their most admired managers to grant a certain level of autonomy in the authority relationship. The worst managers are generally described as the opposite of each of these themes: unresponsive, selfish, insecure, manipulative, and in dire need of people skills. I have obtained very similar response patterns from participants in management development seminars in companies.

After many years of engaging in these discussions, I thought it would be interesting to more systematically collect and document the ideas and stories. After teaching thousands of students over the years, the idea came to me that few cohorts could better articulate their reactions to bosses than the alumni of a business university who had likely worked for numerous managers in varying capacities. In structuring a qualitative study, I arranged to reach out to this population with an electronic survey that simply asked respondents to describe and, if possible, provide a story or narrative about their best and worst managers. The survey also asked for some basic demographic information such as the respondent's gender, the gender of the manager, length of time with the manager, and business or industry category. I explained in the email that accompanied the survey that the study was completely confidential, that all responses would be anonymous and that no names of people or companies would be revealed in the results, although selected excerpts from individual responses might be used as illustrations.[1]

Method

Within a few weeks, the survey yielded a total of 1,058 responses. Each response to the "best" and "worst" managers was recorded verbatim into a secure database along with the demographic information for each respondent. No respondent names or any other identifying information were recorded. In keeping with a qualitative study methodology, the first step was to simply read each response and note the common emerging themes that were recorded in the form of key words or phrases in the descriptions and narratives about the best and worst manager.

After all of the data were read and noted according to emerging themes, the responses were then analyzed in greater depth by applying textual analysis.[2] This search software uses linguistic technologies to sort and extract the data according to frequently mentioned key words and phrases. The program indicates how many individual responses (or cases) contain a root word or phrase (such as *trust* or *communication*) in both the "best" and "worst" manager categories. Sometimes the program also identifies different usages or synonyms (i.e. trusting, trustworthy) in keeping with a particular idea thread. In some cases a key word or phrase was injected into the textual search based on the original reading and coding of responses to see how many times it was mentioned in the responses. The program then identifies the particular case in which the theme appeared so that the researcher can see it in the context of the narrative or general ideas expressed.[3] The procedure is iterative and admittedly more art than science; however, over time one begins to understand and interpret meaningful patterns in the responses. Once the main ideas and themes were established, the data could then be examined taking into account some demographic information, such as gender of respondents and managers, the amount of time spent with the managers, and type of business or organization.

Results

Based on the textual analysis, the words and phrases used by respondents in describing their best managers are listed in Table 2.1 in descending order along with the number and percentage of cases (out of 1,058 total) in which they appear.

By contrast, the results for worst managers followed similar themes, although the numbers of cases containing each theme are not quite as compelling (see Table 2.2).

It is important to keep in mind that these were words, phrases, and themes that were extracted from the respondents' open-ended comments about their experiences with their managers. The respondents were not specifically asked or otherwise prompted to comment on issues such as how their manager served as a mentor or how trustworthy or honest they were. Also, these behavioral themes are not necessarily discrete entities, as multiple themes such as *trust* and *respect* sometimes appeared together in the same cases as *mentor* or *micro-manager*.

TABLE 2.1. Best Manager Themes

Theme	n	%
Mentor/teacher	329	31
Support	198	19
Autonomy	182	17
Respect	144	14
Trust	132	12
Listen	112	11
Open	106	10
Communication	104	10
Feedback	97	9
Fair	77	7
Honest	68	6
Relationship	49	5

TABLE 2.2. Worst Manager Themes

Theme	n	%
Micro-manager	164	16
Communication (poor)	104	10
Disrespect	89	8
Takes credit	73	7
Trust (lack of)	70	7
Feedback (lack of)	56	5
Condescending	50	5
Listening (poor)	46	4
Blames	36	3
Plays favorites	30	3
Insecure	24	2
Dishonest	18	2
Incompetent	12	1

Discussion

Viewing the pattern of responses, it is evident that the *manager as teacher and mentor* is the predominant theme in the best managers and occurred in nearly a third of the total responses. The accompanying themes of *support, autonomy* (expressed as not *micro-managing*), *respect*, and *trust* were clearly in keeping with the overall developmental theme. The best managers also displayed skills in *listening, communicating and providing feedback* in the context of a *fair and honest* working environment. There were compelling stories of these managers creating learning opportunities for their employees, and showing great concern and support for their professional development. The worst managers, on the other hand, were most often described as overbearing *micro-managers* who stifled individual initiative, creativity, and growth. They also betrayed or undermined the fundamental relationship through their actions or inaction. The general themes of *autonomy* (expressed by the use of the term *micro-manager*), *respectful behavior, listening, trustworthiness, feedback, honesty, quality of communication*, and *fairness* (expressed also as playing favorites or taking credit) were themes that factored into both best and worst manager perceptions. It is noteworthy how the respondents focused more on the humanity (or, in some cases, inhumanity) of their managers. Respondents did not seem to focus very much on the general competence of their managers as a source of either satisfaction or frustration in their experience as *incompetence* was specifically mentioned in only 12 cases. Few respondents noted technical knowledge or proficiency in their given field when describing their worst manager. If managers were considered brilliant or knowledgeable business partners, it was always within the context of how well they shared their expertise and enabled their employees to learn from them.

It appears from this analysis that emotional intelligence trumped cognitive intelligence in both categories. Although there are relatively few comprehensive research studies that have tracked the everyday behavior of managers, the findings in this study are consistent with other similar studies of managerial behavior. Based on a Gallup survey of 80,000 managers, Marcus Buckingham and Curt Coffman found that the best managers treat every employee as a unique individual, and focus on enhancing strengths rather than correcting weaknesses. They define the desired outcomes and allow the employee to find the way there, provide the right tools to get the job done, give good and useful feedback, and care about the employee's development as a person.[4] While not a scientific study, another general survey of what makes a "good" boss conducted by Yahoo! HotJobs,[5] indicated these top ten aspects:

1 communication/listening skills
2 effective leadership skills
3 trust in employees to do their jobs well
4 flexibility and understanding
5 intelligence
6 teamwork skills and even temperament (tie)
7 interest in employee development
8 ability to share credit
9 successful in finding and retaining new talent
10 presentation skills.

One frequently mentioned study of top executives conducted by the Center for Creative Leadership found that executives who "derailed" were characterized by two major themes:

1 *rigidity* – the inability to adapt their style to changes in the organizational culture or to take in or respond to feedback about their behavior; and
2 *poor relationships* – being too harshly critical, insensitive or demanding to the point of alienating those with whom they worked. The study also mentioned aspects such as defensiveness and passing blame, trying to get ahead at the expense of others, and abrasive and arrogant communication.[6]

A more recent study focused on the behavior of successful plant managers and also used a qualitative method of determining the themes underlying their behavior. The researchers targeted award-winning plants (such as Baldridge awards and *Industry Week* top plants lists) and interviewed the managers of these highly successful plants. Their analysis revealed a pattern of four core values that served as the underlying themes of their behavior:

1   we value people (valuing and respecting workers, care for their growth and development, mentoring);
2   we value openness (being visible and accessible to workers, communicating, soliciting feedback);
3   we value being positive (creating a positive atmosphere, conscious efforts to boost morale);
4   we value being part of the community (the relationship between the plant and the larger external community, participating in community activities).[7]

Finally, Google recently conducted an internal study called Project Oxygen that statistically analyzed over 10,000 observations of manager behavior across 100 variables taken from performance reviews, surveys, and other reports. The major finding was that employees valued bosses who were even-keeled, held one-on-one meetings, helped their people solve problems by asking questions and not dictating answers, and who took a genuine interest in their lives and careers.[8]

A Deeper Look: The Effects of Gender

When the survey responses were segmented by gender, several interesting patterns emerged. Although the respondents were more or less evenly distributed according to gender (540 males and 506 females in the total group of respondents), their managers were mostly male.[9] Seventy-one percent of the "best" managers and 64 percent of the "worst" managers were male, highlighting the fact that most of the respondents had a greater proportion of male bosses (see Table A.1 in the Appendix), with males showing a bit of an edge as best managers. More interesting is the finding that male respondents overwhelmingly indicated males as their best managers (85 percent) while female respondents were comparatively more even in their allocation of responses between males and females as their best managers (56 and 44 percent respectively), although they also leaned toward males in this category. This same pattern was also observed for the worst managers, although not quite as pronounced for male respondents as 73 percent of males designated a male as their worst manager. Once again, female respondents were more even in their distribution of male and female worst managers (53 percent male, and 47 percent female).

Next, the data were examined according to each of the predominant themes from the textual analysis in relation to gender of the *manager*. The question is: were differences observed in the patterns of themes (or the emphasis on particular attributes) for male and female managers in both best and worst categories? For example, did the emergence of the theme of *mentor-teacher* for best managers differ depending on whether or not the manager was male or female? To get at this result, we examine the *proportion* of responses attributing a particular theme to the gender of the manager (measured as the percentage of responses about male or female managers in relation to the total number of male or female managers). Here, the results were remarkably consistent across gender. The response patterns for the themes in descending order for descriptions of male and female managers appear as follows (see Table 2.3).

As an example, the theme of *mentor-teacher* appeared in 97 cases involving descriptions of a female best manager (or 32 percent of all female best managers), and nearly the identical proportion (31 percent) appeared for descriptions of male best managers (see Table A.10). The theme of *open* appears higher on the list for female best managers as does *listening* for male best managers. Otherwise the patterns are very consistent across gender of the manager. Similar patterns held with perceptions of worst managers.

TABLE 2.3. Manager Themes by Gender

Female Best Managers	Male Best Managers	Female Worst Managers	Male Worst Managers
Mentor/teacher	Mentor/teacher	Micro-manager	Micro-manager
Autonomy	Support	Communication (poor)	Communication (poor)
Support	Autonomy	Disrespect	Disrespect
Respect	Respect	Takes credit*	Takes credit
Open	Trustworthy	Untrustworthy*	Untrustworthy
Trustworthy	Listening	Condescending	Feedback (lack of)
Feedback	Communication	Feedback (lack of)	Listening (poor)
Communication	Open	Blame	Condescending
Listening	Feedback	Plays favorites	Blame
Fair	Fair	Listening (poor)*	Insecure
Honest	Honest	Insecure*	Plays favorites
Relationship	Relationship	Incompetent	Dishonest
		Dishonest	Incompetent

Note
* tie.

The predominant theme of *micro-manager* was mentioned in 17 percent of the cases attributed to female worst managers and in 15 percent of those for male worst managers (see Table A.11). Descriptions of male worst managers tended to place greater emphasis on *poor listening*, and *condescending* appears higher in the order for female worst managers. Apparently respondents were slightly more sensitive to male managers who do not listen well, and reacted more negatively to displays of arrogance or condescending attitudes in women managers.

Overall, while there were some differences attributable to gender, especially regarding how males and female respondents viewed their managers, the underlying themes that form the behavior of these managers are remarkably consistent for both male and female managers. In attempting to explain these patterns, it is possible that male respondents related more to male managers in general and thus focused on males as the best and worst, while female respondents focused more on the actual behavior that they experienced regardless of gender, as they were more evenhanded in both best and worst categories.

Researchers who have studied the effects of gender in the workplace find that men generally view their experiences through more of a *status lens*, in effect asking the question, "am I 'one-up' or 'one down'?" while women view organizational life through more of a *connection lens* and focus on the quality of relationships.[10] In the workplace, men tend to be more direct in their conversation while women are more apt to emphasize politeness. Men tend to dominate discussions during meetings and are more likely to interrupt others. Women tend to prefer to work out solutions with another person while men prefer to work on problems themselves. Finally, women are more likely to downplay their certainty in comparison to men who are more likely to minimize their doubts.[11] Because the narratives in the study contained such strong relationship themes, female respondents were particularly sensitive to these ideas across both male and female managers. It is also possible that female respondents may have held jobs where they were exposed more to both male and female managers, and could make a more even comparison.

At the same time, the distinctions depicted here are comparably small and reinforce the idea that despite much of the popular and comedic material highlighting the gulf of understanding between men and women, the differences are more about nuances of behavior and patterns of conversation rather than fundamental natures. I have often reminded students in my classes that instead of viewing men and women as being from different planets, we live on the same planet, but act on different worldviews and cultural conventions influenced by gender. As the cognitive psychologist Steven Pinker concluded:

> So men are not from Mars, nor are women from Venus. Men and women are from Africa, the cradle of our evolution, where they evolved together

as a single species. Men and women have all the same genes except for a handful on the Y chromosome, and their brains are so similar that it takes an eagle-eyed neuro-anatomist to find the small differences between them. Their average levels of general intelligence are the same, according to the best psychometric estimates, and they use language and think about the physical and living world in the same general way. They feel the same basic emotions, and both enjoy sex, seek intelligent and kind marriage partners, get jealous, make sacrifices for their children, compete for status and mates, and sometimes commit aggression in pursuit of their interests.[12]

What About Performance?

One question often asked about the identification of "best" managers is, how does the behavior of these managers affect performance and productivity? Isn't it possible that the more hard-nosed taskmasters or even micro-managers might extract more work and thus higher productivity in their employees, as unpleasant as working for them might be? Who cares how the results were achieved as long as the goals are met and exceeded? It's a fair question and one of particular saliency given current economic challenges. It is also a question that has been raised in the academic study of leadership. As Dave Ulrich and his associates observe, "In the search for effective leadership, something has often been overlooked. Being capable and possessing the attributes of leadership is terrific, but capability must be put to appropriate, purposeful use."[13] Their multiplicative formula, *Effective leadership = Attributes × Results*, implies that leaders must strive for both components simultaneously and that one should not be forsaken for the other. They provide compelling arguments against the "achieve results at all costs" (including personal costs) philosophy that reinforces the short-term orientation of many firms. They argue that it is important to focus on sustainable results as well as how these results are achieved, and the leader must provide the connection.

Although this study was not structured to directly measure productivity, there are numerous hints in the narratives that the GEMs as defined facilitated better work. There is also a considerable body of research that demonstrates that the kinds of behaviors attributed to these managers are linked with higher productivity. For example, there is evidence that partners in an accounting firm who demonstrated a combination of self-management and social skills dramatically increased profits of the firm, in some cases up to 390 percent incremental profit. Managerial competencies that were shown to distinguish superior performers from average ones include such items as achievement drive, developing others, adaptability, influence, and leadership.[14] Considering that almost half (46 percent) of the best and worst managers depicted in the current study were in the financial, public accounting, and information technology industries, consistent across male and female managers, such performance findings are particularly salient.

One significant performance indicator that did surface more directly in this study was employee turnover. It is often said that employees don't leave organizations; rather, they leave people. Overall, respondents tended to stay with their best managers on average a year longer than their worst managers (3.73 vs. 2.72 years, see Table A.3) and that pattern was almost exactly the same across male and female respondents. As will be seen in the narratives in the coming chapters, there were frequent stories that ended with an employee leaving an intolerable situation or of an ineffective boss being terminated or moved to another position in the firm. The more frequent loss of employees carries a significant cost to companies in the form of: lost productivity during the time of acquiring new staff (estimated as two months of sales or production costs or one-third of a new employee's first year salary); lower productivity during the learning curve phase of a new hire; and the out-of-pocket direct costs for relocation and training as part of replacing a professional employee.[15] While direct costs are not available in this study, there is evidence that the perceived best managers created a more stable and perhaps more productive work environment.

Conclusions

Viewing the above results as a whole, we may conclude that the best managers:

1 *serve as mentors, teachers and supporters* of their employees, allowing sufficient autonomy and room to grow and develop;
2 *build and maintain effective relationships* on a foundation of trust and respect by listening well, communicating clearly, providing helpful feedback, and remaining open to new ideas;
3 *manage with high levels of integrity*, characterized by honesty, fairness, humility, and ethical behavior.

The most compelling finding is that the data largely confirm the overarching idea that the "best" managers are actually "good enough managers" as themes in both best and worst categories indicate that the perceived best managers (or GEMs) created a teaching or *facilitating* relationship characterized by autonomy, responsive support and development. These managers were also able to acknowledge their limitations and shortcomings without blaming others or taking credit where it was not due. The worst managers, primarily described as "micro-managers," often undermined these relationships. In the following chapters, these major good enough themes will be explored in much greater depth, drawing upon the respondents' descriptions and narratives that give life to these findings.

three

GEMs as Mentors and Teachers

The only fuel for learning is the sadness you feel from your mistakes. It's important not to waste this fuel.

—Elvin Semrad

Tacked to the cork bulletin board in my office is a faded handwritten quote given to me by a student over 25 years ago, stating that "a great teacher is not one who imparts knowledge to students, but one who awakens their interest in it and makes them eager to pursue it for themselves."[1] I have been a teacher for over 30 years and have tried to live by this philosophy. I am often asked how I came to my philosophy and style as a teacher and I immediately respond that I did not learn to teach through my college or graduate school curricula. My graduate training prepared me to be a scholar in my field, but the inspiration to teach was something that was planted in me through a variety of experiences dating back to my early childhood.

I grew up in a small town in North Carolina and many of my earliest memories involve my family's business, a men's clothing store that was established by my Russian immigrant grandfather in the early 1900s, and continued by my father and uncle for many years. They had a particularly personal way of interacting with their customers, long preceding current interests in customer-focused management that was an embodiment of small town life. Many of the southern gentlemen in our town knew my father and uncle well for many years, some since childhood, and enjoyed their humor and stories as much as the merchandise. They came for the human experience, knowing that their tastes and preferences would be honored, and that the selling would never be rushed or pushed. Occasionally my uncle would introduce a new color or style, but always in keeping with the customer's general outlook and sensibility. As a young boy I was often perplexed about why these men would drop in on a regular basis just to talk, exchange jokes, stories, and news of the town; but I grew to realize that it was all about the relationships that encompassed the sales. Something meaningful transpired in that small corner of the world. Though lacking in formal education themselves, in their own unique way, my father and uncle were teachers who educated their customers as they developed and nurtured a regular and loyal clientele. Selling was a persuasive performance as they engaged in a very human exchange with their clients, who walked away with more than merchandise. They felt valued as human beings. As a result my family seldom formally advertised as customers knew where to go for clothing and the welcoming atmosphere. Their particular interpersonal style and underlying values enhanced and reinforced by my mother's value of formal education, and the behavior of influential teachers from elementary school on through my doctoral program, contributed greatly to my desire to teach and eventual approach and style of teaching.

The study documented in the previous chapter highlighted the fact that managers who served a teaching and developmental role for their employees were most highly regarded. Management scholars have noted that there is a significant teaching role in managing. Recalling that the original Mentor was the trusted advisor to the classical figures Odysseus and his son, Telemachus, Harry Levinson identifies the "mentor alliance" in which the manager as teacher serves as a role model who shapes his/her protégé by *following the grain* of their strengths and talents in the manner of a sculptor, rather than forcing them into a preconceived model.[2] As in the best teaching relationships, the learning is mutual. Mentoring follows a developmental progression. We take on different mentors as we move through life and career stages, ideally forming a network of mentors that can function like a personal board of directors.[3] However it occurs, the most important aspect is the learning relationship that touches the core of who we are and where we want to go in our careers and life.

Parker Palmer states that the power of the teacher as a mentor is in his or her capacity to awaken a truth within us that can be recalled years later, just as I remembered my early experiences with my father and uncle.[4] This kind of mentoring relationship is based on two inter-related processes:

1 *identification* – absorbing and internalizing the characteristics, values, and behavior of key figures in our lives; and
2 *integrity* – integrating the various experiences into a meaningful whole to form a distinct understanding of the self.

The revelation that over one-third of the responses about "best" managers centered on the theme of the manager as mentor and teacher provides a strong statement about this central facet of managing. Many stories high-lighted a powerful mentor relationship that enabled employees to learn and grow on the job, as illustrated by the following excerpts:

> My best manager/mentor knew how to strike the perfect balance between being my manager and being my mentor. After time, I could confide in this person, but I also had no inclinations to "push my luck" and take advantage of our professional relationship. He had a strict motto to treat all of his subordinates as "people with souls," and treated everyone with respect.

> My best boss was the CEO at my previous company. He was a pure entrepreneur that had built the company over a period of 20 years. His decision making process was based on his instincts, as opposed to mine which was based upon detailed analysis and risk/reward evaluation. The reason I believe that he was my best boss is that he saw potential in me that I did not see in myself. He pushed and prodded me to do things that I did not believe I was capable of. He was always right in believing I could do something and I learned to trust his instincts even when I thought that he was expecting me to achieve the impossible. The lessons I learned from him were that we are capable of doing things we thought we couldn't. I also learned to always trust my instincts.

> The theory behind the best and most effective manager I have had in my ten years since graduating was her idea that when I looked good, she looked good. Therefore, she put time into training me throughout the two years I worked for her in not only the technical knowledge I needed to have in the role, but also offered the experience I needed to ensure that in due time I would be able to "fly on my own" in presentations and meeting with clients.

We see in these descriptions a balance between the personal and professional, the personal discovery of one's potential and the ability to trust one's instincts, and the value of careful training for mutual benefit so that a thoroughly prepared employee can eventually "fly the nest."

Winnicott referred to this fundamental relationship as a "good enough facilitating environment."[5] This relationship is the human mechanism that creates a path to mature development and growth as a professional. As noted in the following case examples, the GEMs are the *facilitators* who provide clear direction, guidance, and feedback, and promote and elicit learning in their employees so that the work gets done and people grow along the way. Here are a few more examples with teaching and learning as central themes:

When I look around at the next step in my career, I look at my current management team and I know that when I reach their level I would want to mimic their style and level of expertise. My boss is someone who has helped me further develop my skill-set, has given me the opportunity to take on responsibility outside of my role and the most important thing is I know that I always have his support. He is hands on when I ask him to be, but he also gives me room to figure issues/solutions out on my own. He is a master motivator and someone who, if he left this company, I would follow elsewhere. He coaches me on topics outside of my knowledge base and encourages me to think for myself.

The best manager or boss with whom I have worked was a coach; a mentor. Assignments were given, parameters outlined, and then I was left on my own; checking in with questions and outlining my approach, progress, etc. until project completed. For example, I was assigned to review a system and recommend a more efficient procedure. I was always introduced and told about those I would be working with; told a little about the present procedures and the need for greater efficiency. As I worked, and problems arose I was able to question my boss and decide on approaches to be taken. Results were such that they were not my changes, but ones the people who worked the system recommended and approved. It made the work a pleasure to perform and the results successfully carried out. This boss made you feel capable, in charge and trusted.

Notice the level of give and take in these stories as the managers set the tone that employees wished to emulate, mimic, and follow. They were motivators and supportive coaches who instilled confidence and enhanced proficiency. Of the more than 1,000 stories generated by the study, most respondents focused on the interpersonal interactions with their bosses, often noting how the best ones were attentive to their needs and inevitable shortcomings while at the same time giving them room to find their own way.

Autonomy Within Established Boundaries

Winnicott's central notion of autonomy within boundaries that forms the early "holding environment" was clearly present in several reflections. *Autonomy* was a notable theme running through descriptions of the best managers as was its opposite, *micro-managing*, with perceptions of the worst. Autonomy is a significant component of employee motivation and job satisfaction dating back to the original "job enrichment" studies of the early 1970s.[6] It has found a new footing in more modern discussions about management. As Daniel

Pink states, human beings were meant to be players, not pawns, and cites autonomy as a key feature of "future facing" twenty-first century companies such as FedEx and Google. He presents four essential domains of autonomy:

1   what people do (autonomy over the *task*)
2   when they do it (autonomy over *time*)
3   how they do it (autonomy over *technique)*
4   with whom they do it (autonomy over their *team*).

According to Pink, we can learn a lot about autonomy from artists such as Picasso, Georgia O'Keeffe, and Jackson Pollock. No one told them when to paint or to use a specific technique with assigned assistants to work with them. These artists created masterpieces in their own way, exercised self-control, yet were ultimately accountable for their work.[7]

The same philosophy is finding its way into corporate life in the form of results only work environments (ROWE) and organizations tailored more to the individual talents and desires of employees.[8] Autonomy and its varying forms, such as self-managing work teams, have softened the rigid hierarchies of the industrial age when it was more common practice for a person, usually a young man, to spend his entire career in one company and work his way up the corporate ladder from the mailroom to the executive suite. The transformation to more information-based work accompanied by vast improvements in technology, has resulted in more organic and fluid structures that have replaced the command and control hierarchy along with providing greater amounts of autonomy.

Just because hierarchies are less calcified does not mean that hierarchies have disappeared or are less important. In fact, there is considerable psychological research that shows that social hierarchies, even in egalitarian societies, are crucial to organizational stability and individual identity. Like other social animals such as wolves and primates, humans naturally create social rankings and are more comfortable and productive when they operate within the established order, especially when situated lower in the social order; it is a way of keeping order and preserving the social group, a complex and deeply held evolutionary impulse.[9] This is why the increasingly common practice of giving every kid on the soccer or little league team a trophy often rings hollow and makes such well-intentioned "everyone's a winner" awards meaningless and plays into our obsession with perfection. The recognition of hierarchy does not automatically translate into unquestioned and blind obedience to authority or the perpetuation of institutionally sanctioned inequality. Likewise, autonomy is not simply turning employees loose; rather, it is more of a negotiated balance between independence and control, otherwise known as *interdependence*. Autonomy and authority are not mutually exclusive. They work together.

The GEMs in the study seemed to strike the right balance between holding on and letting go as depicted in the following employee descriptions:

> My best manager earned that distinction by giving me the space I needed to do my job "my way" while being close enough to support me and provide help so I didn't fail. That line between close enough but not too close is a fine one, and the ability to do that requires excellent people skills and evaluation skills.... My boss once put me in charge of a systems project that would ultimately provide an operations system to a group of users. My boss let me run meetings, plan strategy, determine schedules and manage staff to make the project successful. He met with me weekly, and as I needed, without being present at project meetings. When I felt the project/system was ready, the operations manager disagreed. I had test results and project documentation to provide proof of readiness. My boss backed me 100% and gave the go ahead to install the system, which was successful. He was my best manager because of how he managed me, but even more important, he was my best manager because he demonstrated to me how to be a good manager, and I owe a great deal of my success as a manager/leader to him.

> The best boss I've had was focused, brilliant, communicative, available, dynamic, energetic, and creative. He also recognized how individuals needed to be managed. So, he could be "big daddy" when necessary or give independence to those who could handle [it]. To turn a business unit around, he hired a team of very big personalities. In less adept hands, the politics and ambitions could have prevented progress. Everyone stayed so focused on the goal we hit it.

> I really believe the person I would consider my best manager would be the one that gave me the greatest autonomy. He empowered me to make decisions for the area of responsibility that I had and trusted me to make the right decisions. He always supported my decisions and would listen to new ideas that I had, encouraging me to try them rather than saying, "Oh that will never work." He also would send me little handwritten notes every once in a while that recognized the work that I did. He was selfless in his need for recognition and always said, "If you look good, then I look good." I always appreciated his confidence in me.

> She doesn't hold my hand, but doesn't throw me into the fire either as I am still new. I currently have the perfect balance of independence and support. Also, I appreciate her feedback whether it was positive or constructive, as I value honesty in all of my relationships.

He is the best because he leads with his heart. He takes the time to build deep relationships with people. He understands his people well, gives meaningful participation and rewards them [with] loyalty. He expects the same in return. He shows patience and support but is direct and holds me accountable to standards that are high ... just like he holds himself accountable to those same standards. He is in the detail, yet has great vision, is dynamic and has great overall business skills. When he assumed his current job he personally visited all 72 of our field locations and did a personal one-on-one sharing [of] his story with over 100 managers across the US.

The best manager that I have worked with was hands off enough to let me develop but hands on enough so that I knew that if I needed her she would be there to help me. By allowing me to complete projects on my own not only inspired me to work harder, because I wanted to retain her confidence in my abilities, but it also helped me to develop confidence in my own work. She was also approachable and allowed me to ask questions of her in a manner where I did not feel I was being judged, every question was treated as important and she always made sure to walk me through how she reasoned out the conclusion. She allowed me to grow through my hard work and never tried to pass off my work as her own. This furthered my career within the company as others began to take my work more seriously and I was allowed to take on more challenging jobs. I believe that we worked well together because she took the time to figure out what motivated me and she made sure to work with me in that way. The constant communication also made me feel comfortable in approaching her and I believe made her comfortable that the work was being done.

Employees in these stories experienced both autonomy and support, but also had the experience of working within a well-established structure. Boundaries form and define relationships from the earliest stages and remain important throughout our lives. As Ed Shapiro and Wesley Carr state, "When parents ask their child, 'What is your experience?' they authorize the child to *have* a separate experience," thus forming a boundary between parent and child.[10] This early boundary is essential to healthy growth and development, creating a sense of self-awareness important to building good future relationships.

Robert Frost poetically stated, "Good fences make good neighbors." Most creatures, animal and human, are aware of their territory and its limits, and tend to seek and respond to boundaries. Before a game is played, we usually ask, "What are the rules?" All sports make the distinction between an action that is "fair" or "out of bounds," whether it is the foul ball or home run in baseball, the bordered grid of the football or soccer field, the basketball court or the roped lines of the boxing ring. We become uncomfortable when the game spills out into the stands as was the case when basketball star Ron Artest famously leapt into the crowd during a game and began fighting with someone who had been taunting him.[11] In the same way, we are not particularly appreciative of the overzealous fan that runs onto the field and tries to tackle an opposing player or enjoy a moment in the spotlight before being arrested. The television networks now divert their cameras so as not to encourage such trespassing. The short-lived XFL (extreme football) was widely panned by true football fans because the commonly understood rules were relaxed to make it more "exciting" for viewers. It failed miserably, especially among football purists who saw it as an abomination and a violation of the integrity of the game. Our laws, rules, and regulations define the limits of our behavior in relation to our culture, community, and in our personal relationships. Certain individuals such as referees, law enforcement agents, and judges are designated as the keepers of these boundaries and make the calls that interpret, reinforce and, at times, refine them. We may not like all the calls, but we like the fact that the calls are made.

Boundaries serve to separate a social system from its external environment and establish the lines of demarcation between what is inside and what remains outside.[12] The very idea of an organization sets out a system of transacting boundaries in the form of structure, design, tasks, and roles that define and contain the human experiences within them, including both individual and group dynamics. Those who occupy the role of manager are those who are often entrusted with creating, maintaining, and navigating these boundaries in the form of defining goals and expectations, monitoring the environment, tasks and workflow, evaluating performance, and communicating the rules by which work will be done. As with the appreciation of social hierarchies described above, employees as human beings both expect and respect such boundaries. Boundaries also serve to contain powerful emotions and allow managers to provide perspective for their employees by enabling them to have their own experiences in relation to the work being accomplished, as shown in the following description from a younger employee:

> The best manager I worked for was one who gave me autonomy and trusted me to perform. At first I had to prove myself and my capabilities because he had assumptions based on my age and lack of experience. I did this by consistently performing at a level that exceeded his expectations. When my boss gave me tasks, he framed them by sharing a vision and goal. He did not give step by step instructions. Instead, he gave me the goal and set the guardrails – or boundaries. If I ever got close to a guardrail, he made it comfortable to approach him with questions.

Instead of giving me the answer, he would ask more questions so that I could think up a solution myself. If I was performing fine (within the guardrails) my boss would trust me to execute on the vision or achieve the goal.

Risk and Safety

Boundaries also present a challenge. The writer James Carroll noted that when boundaries get blurred in the natural world, such as when floods and fires bring animals into more direct contact with humans or when diseases, such as HIV/AIDS or swine flu, jump the boundary between animals and humans, our sense of order breaks down and we fear chaos. Similarly, the economic collapse in 2008 could be seen in part as a breakdown of regulations and the established financial order. Yet, as Carroll also observes,

> it has been humans drawing order out of chaos. Ironically, the boundary-less situations, from what we know of evolution, have been the most creative. Our forebears in life, after all, arose out of the place where water and land made mud. Where the boundary fell between jungle and savannah, we learned to walk upright. Where life met death, our unbound feelings taught us memory and hope. We formed the habit of erecting boundaries to be safe, in sum – but also in order to transcend them.[13]

It is at this edge between order and chaos that the GEMs are most effective. While boundaries help to create a safe environment, the GEMs also seemed to strike the appropriate balance between safety and the risk that enabled their employees to stretch and perhaps even transcend defined limits. As one employee observed:

> The best manager I have ever had provided me with the ability and flexibility to take risks in a "safe" environment. As a result, it provided me with the opportunity for increased exposure, a great learning experience and the ability to develop the skill to ascertain when a risk is calculated and the repercussions.

Along with the foundation of a relatively safe environment come the ability and even the desire to learn from mistakes as was evident in the following episodes:

> This manager provided detailed training when it was needed but took a hands-off approach after you learned the job. He allowed his people to

make mistakes without recrimination. He made every individual feel like a valued member of the team. When I made a $6 million error in preparing a cost estimate for a large project he helped me explain it to the team leader and made it into a learning experience. I was a junior member of the team, yet he had me make presentations directly to upper management.

My best manager was very fair and constructively honest with me. He felt it his duty and obligation to help me move along in my own management career and was always on the lookout for facets of management to teach me and valuable experiences to throw me into. Once, when I really screwed something up in a big way, he simply asked me "What did you learn from this?" rather than freak out or scold. It was very effective – I felt awful and never made the same mistake again. To this day, I work very hard to make mistakes only once, and I am mindful of this experience when my own managers make mistakes (the FIRST time, that is!).

The best manager I ever had encouraged me to do my best without micro-managing in any way. He made me absolutely fearless to try new things in order to improve things. He told me early on in my career with him that he would support me in my job. He said that if I made mistakes, he would take all of the blame, but if I had successes, I would get all of the credit. He then proceeded to do exactly what he said he would. What a safety net!

This question is difficult as the best manager that I have had is actually a combination of two different managers. However, if I were to choose one I would choose the one that assigned work to me and allowed me the freedom to fail. I have learned more under this manager as I have conducted assigned tasks with a higher level of ownership ensuring that I have covered all bases.

I surmise that these managers allowed the "freedom to fail" because they were not threatened by the potential of failure and uncertainty. They were more comfortable letting go of enough control that their employees could take a risk, live with the results, and turn it into a learning experience that ultimately set the stage for even greater creativity. The GEMs seem to instinctively find that tension point where the balance between risk and safety produces something valuable. There is a motivational quality in these responses as employees took ownership of their work and aspired to excellence. It is also interesting that they passed along the same open attitude when it became their time to manage. The following story illustrates how a mistake could be turned into a career opportunity based on the actions of a unique manager:

> I happened to have a lot of experience with a manager that I feel is probably going to be the best manager I will ever have experienced with for the rest of my life. His colleagues described him as a mentor and leader, someone they truly admired. There are countless stories that I could share as to why he was the best manager, and that alone should be another clue that you really are dealing with someone who has remarkable managerial skills. One story that I am particularly fond of is about an employee who made a mistake. Working in a financial industry, employees are constantly dealing with numbers and, as will occur in any industry, mistakes will sometimes occur. This one employee worked in a different department and the mistake was costly to the company but prior to this situation the employee had given the company no other reason to doubt him. Unfortunately, however, this employee's manager thought this mistake was grounds for firing. As word spread around, my manager became visibly outraged that a good hard worker could be fired over one mistake. At that exact moment, he walked over to the desk of the employee as he was packing up his items and hired him on the spot to work under him. That particular employee became one of his hardest working and the rest of us learned a lot about what it means to work for someone who puts their employees first. As I was writing that story a dozen or so more stories popped into my head. One that really gave the employees the feeling of security and motivation was the knowledge that he would not downsize our department. He never shared this information with any of us but it was known that he refused to lay people off regardless of what the company wanted from him instead saying he would fire himself first. I know that he was with the company for over 30 years and his was the only department during that time period to not lay anyone off because the company needed to downsize. He had courage, leadership, unbreakable values, the ability to listen and to be able to solve any situation, both work related and personal, you could possibly have.

Granted, these are exceptional managers and rare experiences, but the stories show that real GEMs go out of their way and even put themselves on the line to benefit their employees.

It's Not All "Touchy-Feely"

The study and appreciation of interpersonal relations and emotional intelligence often leads to stereotypes of a manager who is a saint: a cross between

Mother Teresa and the Dalai Lama. *Holding* in this sense can be mistaken for "hand holding" and that is not always the case. As Daniel Goleman and others have noted, being emotionally intelligent cannot be reduced to just "being nice." I'm sure that many of these GEMs are nice people who treat their workers well and care deeply about them as people, but managing effectively often requires conflict, confrontation, and just plain hard work. The best managers, while responsive and supportive of their employees, also held very high standards and sometimes showed sharper edges, but always in the context of a learning and supportive relationship. In the following descriptions we see two very effective managerial relationships where employees are challenged, held to high standards, and different views are integrated:

> One boss that I qualify as a good boss is one who had been my manager in an IT project. He actually was not gentle as a human, but he had coached me well. He gave me autonomy, and was there to answer my questions when I needed that. He also provided very good advice and I remember that he always encouraged me by giving me a margin of error. In a way I felt safe doing my work, despite the fact that he and I had big personality differences that can't be reconciled. But still it was a good professional relationship and we succeeded in our work project.

> I currently work for my best manager and enjoy working for him so much that I have recently followed him to another department. He makes me feel valued by seeking out and listening to my point of view and empowered by allowing me to do my job my way (i.e. he does not micro manage me). He sets challenging objectives for me that allow me to grow and learn and clearly outlines expectations for performance. He provides timely and constructive feedback and is open to receiving the same. He rewards accomplishments and is willing to share the spotlight and he holds me, and others, accountable when expectations are not met – great motivator. The above ensures my annual reviews are never a surprise. We typically come to the same conclusions about my performance for the prior year, what my strengths are and where I could improve. He lays out the vision for the department illustrating how it links back to the division and company objectives and in turn how it links my objectives. I may not always agree with him but he is consistent and fair which makes accepting a different point of view easier. He is also a great coach. He has helped me to become a better manager. Example – when it came time to eliminate a position within our department he allowed me to be the one to have the conversation with the employee even though senior management felt he should be the one having the conversation. He knew this would be a good, albeit, painful experience for me

and one that I would need to progress as a manager. He coached me through the process and made sure I had the support I needed from other departments. I can think of many examples for this manager but ultimately it is his consistent behavior and leadership that gives me the overall feeling of being valued and empowered. In my opinion this is why he is my best manager.

Most of us can recall the teacher or coach that exhibited the "tough love" that drove us to new heights of performance. They weren't always easy to deal with, but somehow we sensed (or maybe realized in retrospect) that they had our best interests in mind. Mine was Miss Jenkins, my eighth grade English teacher. Although she was scarcely five feet tall, her voice alone would strike fear in all of us, a fear that was enshrined across generations of students that came before. Her thorough critiques of our writing were at times withering, caustic, and laced with her famous aphorisms "You missed the boat" and "You're out to lunch," delivered in the most dismissive of tones, hilarious to 13-year-olds in the 1960s, and that today could invite a lawsuit for bruising fragile young egos. She was demanding and maintained clear boundaries and high expectations of performance, yet one could sense the twinkle in her eye when she would let loose with one of her "tirades," knowing – perhaps unconsciously – that she loved her students despite their foibles and struggles and was totally dedicated to their learning. Within those boundaries of subjects, predicates, and dangling participles placed in elegantly diagrammed sentences I wrote an award-winning historical essay on the founding of the University of North Carolina that paved my eventual path to that very institution. Her editorial presence pervades each sentence that I write to this day.

The Anti-GEM: Beware the Micro-Manager

Then there are those managers for whom boundaries become rigid walls. Rather than shaping and sculpting, these bosses apparently are more concerned with controlling and preserving their own power.

The worst manager I had was an emotional micromanager that was prone to explosive outbursts, belittling sarcasm and a tempestuous insecurity. Though technically brilliant, this manager was a sole contributor, who did not understand how to motivate or how to encourage.

My worst boss gave me absolutely no control over my own schedule, and had no consideration for my own personal or professional obligations. For instance, he once dumped a very complicated assignment on my desk on a Friday afternoon, informing me that he would be in New Mexico and unreachable for the weekend. I e-mailed him the project once it was complete, only to have the "unreachable" boss phone me and gleefully detail all of the problems with the job I had done and how much more work I'd have to put in to "fix" it.

Coincidently, I've just recently worked for (and resigned from) the worst manager I've ever had. He is the President of a very successful family-owned business. I was brought on as COO to bring the company to the "next level." Not long after I "quantum-leaped" I knew I had made a mistake (oh boy). He was extremely abusive to employees at all levels of the organization; from the Call Center customer service reps to the V.P. of Sales. He would dress people down in front of all others. He would walk out of a meeting as soon as you started to disagree with him. His incentive pay was completely arbitrary. He micro-managed like you read about. He traumatized most everyone in the organization. You felt as though any day could be your last. He read the latest management books and periodicals and then half-implemented the recommendations that supported his preconceived notions. He was abusive to vendors. His is the type of behavior that inspires coup d'état and writers of comic strips like Dilbert. He was the absolute antithesis of the best manager I ever had.

Antithesis indeed! One of the best ways to fully appreciate the GEMs is to probe their opposite. The most frequently mentioned term applied to the worst managers was *micro-manager*, seen in the above descriptions as focused on the trees rather than the forest, combined with behavior that is over-controlling, arbitrary, and, at times but not always, hostile and vindictive. The micro-managers were seen as aversive to risk and thereby stifled creativity, and were emotionally insecure and more interested in meeting their own needs rather than being responsive and open to their employees' ideas, strengths, and feelings. More often than not, according to many narratives, they drove their projects or companies to failure, were fired, or in some other way removed from their position.

What is most striking is how diametrically opposite they are in contrast to the GEMs. In many cases they are technically competent, even recognized as brilliant in some instances, yet in the descriptions one senses a fragility underlying their need to control others. Some psychologists would venture to say that the micro-managers, even if well intended, were projecting their own (unacknowledged) vulnerability or insecurity onto their employees. Some may use their employees as scapegoats, as they often were quick to assign blame for any perceived mistake. Perhaps it bolstered their egos or quelled their anxiety as in the following Jekyll/Hyde tale of a "nice guy" who, when under stress, transformed into the *Micro-manager from Hell*:

By opposite contrast, another boss that I had (at a previous job) would yell, berate and try to intimidate everyone (even those not reporting to this person). Many times, the team would be working long hours on projects, getting things done only to have this person tear up the work and call it junk (even if there was not anything wrong with it). Personally, he was a nice guy; however, when he had pressure applied to him, he was horrible. He could not take any type of stress. He would micro-manage every project and yell if things were not done exactly as he thought they should be. He would even change numbers on reports if they were bad or if he did not believe them, even if the math supported the findings (eventually, that was his downfall).

Micro-managing occurred in many situations and in many forms, even showing up in cyberspace. One would think that the flexibility enabled by the growing prevalence of virtual workplaces would increase autonomy, but apparently that is not always the case:

One of the characteristics of my worst managers is micro-managing. One manager used to comment about the time on which I log into the instant messenger as an indication for when I started working. The other manager (for whom I worked remotely) was frustrated that he does not know where I am in any given time and asked me to install a webcam on my desk so he could see me all day.

Finally, we have an example of what may be termed micro-manager *in extremis*:

(She was) a micromanager to the worst extent. (She) asked for a phone call to be made to her on Monday morning at 8:00 am (no earlier or later) to explain where you were going, what you were doing and what you were going to say. By the way, this is after you submitted a weekly call report on Friday for the upcoming week ... with all the information contained in the report. She expected a phone call at 5:30 pm on Monday afternoon rehashing where you went for the day, what you did and said and then you had to explain all the information for Tuesday. She expected a call at 8:00 am on Tuesday morning explaining where you were going, what you were doing and what you were going to say. Then you had to rehash where you went, what was said and what was done on Monday. Did I mention that there was this weekly call report thing? Well this went on every morning and every afternoon hashing and rehashing the information for the week till 5:30 pm on Friday afternoon ... then it started all over again on Monday. I lasted six months.

The micro-managers invited the defensiveness of those working for them, creating the placating and compliant "false self" that Winnicott describes:

> Micro manager. Watched pennies and the dollars flow out the door. Created division amongst employees (and) was secretive. Held a funny tight rein on "need to know" information that was basically immaterial. His manner created an uneasy feeling that led to lack of productivity and made for tremendous turnover.

> He was an experienced operations executive who had moved up to CEO of the company. He was extremely control oriented and assumed that he knew the jobs of all of the functional executives better than they (even though he had no direct experience in their functions). He would involve himself in the details of every function and every decision, almost regardless of decision level. He would reverse the decisions of the senior executives in public forums, and generally caused everyone to develop the attitude that if it was not his idea or had his explicit approval, it was not worth wasting time on it. One meeting of the executives that I recall was cancelled when he was ill and the executives decided to cancel in that they could not make any decisions in his absence, since they would simply be changed or reversed. He used data selectively to support decisions that he had really already made (but depicted as being under discussion), and ignored information that was not in concert with his conclusion. He eventually took the company into bankruptcy and the closing of the company, causing the venture capital investors to lose all of their investment in the company and 6,000 employees to lose their jobs.

Employees in such situations learn not to venture forth with their creative ideas, knowing that they will either be ignored or rejected. This scenario can set up various communication "games," ritualized patterns that serve to obscure and prevent genuine exchanges of ideas. Some of these games take on a persecutory tone, such as the Blamer and the Placater.[14] The Placater goes along to get along in order to keep the micro-managing, fault-finding Blamer off his back; however, this form of passive-aggression can set up the next round of the game as now the players are more intent on winning this little battle, rather than genuinely communicating and getting work done. This gets tiring, especially for highly competent workers. These employees can be caught in a bind in such conditions, trying to defensively go along with what the manager asks, only to have their attempts backfire as in the following stories:

> My worst manager was a "micro-manager." He was unable to delegate responsibility. As the chief financial officer, he was often seen entering

transactions into the general ledger system (despite having a staff of five accountants.) During my performance review he asked me to assess his performance as a manager. I tried to phrase my response as positively as possible and said that I worked best when allowed to work on my own. The following day he presented me with a three page typewritten dissertation on his rationale for working so closely with his staff. I guess he couldn't accept constructive criticism either!

My worst manager was very difficult to work for. He had an incredibly short attention span and struggled to remain focused long enough for me to answer even the most brief questions he asked me. He was an incredible micromanager that did not take the time when he joined our group to determine the backgrounds, education or skill sets of anyone who worked for him. Rather, he assumed that his experience and skill sets were superior and managed accordingly. He did not see the value in taking time to learn the business of the industry he transitioned to, but instead operated as if sales were the same in any industry. His lack of ability and skill was instantly apparent, yet it took our senior level executives six months to realize this and react. I will never forget the first one on one meeting I had with him, where he asked me if I agreed with his philosophy of making calls and closing customers FOR our sales reps, in rapid succession, to "show them how it's done." As our sales force at the time was quite mature and tenured, and as I felt our managers were better served to listen and coach reps AFTER they conclude customer calls, I politely disagreed with him. I said something to the effect of "I'm generally a more empowering type of manager, and I feel our reps can learn more by making their own mistakes and hearing constructive feedback from a good coach..." He quickly cut me off, and in a dramatic change of tone informed me that this would be unacceptable. His words were "I think if you don't agree with me on this, then you are just going to slow me down and get in my way. You are a very nice person and I would be glad to help you find another position within the company." I was pretty shocked, as this was literally his third day in the office. His first week with us was spent at an off-site sales meeting, where I was called out for the highest sales attainment (for my six teams of regional sales managers and reps) for the past quarter. This was the beginning of three grueling months of wondering daily whether or not he would let me go. By the beginning of month four, he openly expressed "awe" at my management ability and grasp of our business, saying he respected me tremendously. The intense and misguided micromanagement never ceased however, and eventually his poor attention to detail and general lack of ability to understand our business caught up with him. He was let go after just six months on the job.

It was interesting that many of the micro-managers were mostly referred to in the past tense as the respondents had happily left them or, as in many destructive or abusive relationships, had stayed longer than necessary:

> I have to say that the things that make my boss the "worst" manager were her micro-management skills and having no confidence in her workers. She often asked us to teach her how to use certain programs on the computer. Some of the things she did were: 1) she frequently comes around the work area and asked us what you are working on. 2) if we stepped out of the office, she wanted to know where we were, etc. I managed to stay there for five years while attending college because of the benefits. The people she hired wouldn't stay for long. Sometimes the people she hired would stay for a few months, or leave at their lunch break and never return.

Like the iconic Chinese symbol, the good enough manager and the micro-manager comprise the *yin* and *yang* of managing in modern organizations. It is tempting to set up the GEM and Micro-Manager as polar opposites, a Manichean choice between "night and day" good and evil management styles, when in fact the differences are more subtle and not that simply drawn. The managers may have more in common than appears on the surface. Both exercise their legitimate authority, feel strong emotions, and have a desire to get the work accomplished in response to external demands. There are times when the attention to detail and close and careful supervision characteristic of the micro-manager are appropriate and even desirable behaviors, such as in crisis situations, or when the employees are inexperienced and need more guidance, consistent with situational leadership theory. Taking the deeper view, the key distinction is that the *good enough managers* are more open and responsive to their employees' needs and the organizational context; they can handle their emotions and let go of their own certitude, and know when to move closer and when to back away. As the shadow of the GEM, the micro-manager is more about managing by certainty where certainty does not exist, springing from a reservoir of often unacknowledged anxiety and insecurity. The GEMs, as teachers and mentors, seem to work best at the edge of the boundary between knowing and not knowing, affirming it yet encouraging their employees to push against and at times transcend it, simultaneously holding on and letting go, *a part of and apart from* their employees' efforts and work lives.

four

GEMs as Relationship Builders

We have so little faith in the ebb and flow of life, of love, of relationships. We leap at the flow of the tide and resist in terror its ebb.... For relationships, too, must be like islands. One must accept them for what they are here and now, within their limits — islands, surrounded and interrupted by the sea, continually visited and abandoned by the tides.

—Anne Morrow Lindbergh

One of the dominant findings of the study was that GEMs created a facilitating work environment by building and nurturing mutually beneficial relationships characterized by trust, respect, and open communication. Since the oft-cited Hawthorne Studies and the rise of the Human Relations School of organizational functioning in the 1940s and 1950s, relationships have been a central aspect of management thought and practice. This human focus flourished during the 1960s with a renewed emphasis on teams, sensitivity training, and organizational development aimed at improving human interaction at work, especially between leaders and subordinates. To fully appreciate these trends, it is important to explore them in the context of larger cultural forces of the latter part of the twentieth century. These more democratic and humanistic trends in management and organizations coincided with larger cultural influences such as the general questioning of authority and established structures, social justice exemplified by the civil rights and women's movements, and the greater emphasis on self-actualization and human potential in psychology.

As we moved into the 1970s, we saw a number of defining cultural markers: the yellow smiley-face, glitter rock and disco music, polyester, and hair and clothing styles of questionable taste and proportions. The events collectively known as the Watergate scandal, along with the energy crisis and runaway inflation, defined a period of growing distrust in institutions, the concern about ethics and the role of government in society, and a gradual rightward turn in politics that ushered in the age of Reagan. The personal computer was just on the horizon, and with it, the first glimmers of the information age.

Also, beginning in 1970, one of the most popular and successful television shows, *The Mary Tyler Moore Show*, epitomized the era in at least two important ways. The central character, Mary Richards, was a single woman "making it on her own" and a symbol of the nascent women's movement. As a situation comedy, the show was set in a workplace and much of the action revolved around the work colleagues who produced a daily news show in Minneapolis. The comedic tension emanated from their relationships with each other and their gruff yet lovable boss, Lou Grant, masterfully played by Ed Asner. As the show progressed over seven seasons, these complex fictional relationships grew and deepened, culminating in the extended group embrace and genuine expression of love among these characters when the station was sold and the characters ended their work together in the final episode. Thus began an era of workplace comedy and drama shows such as *MASH*, *Cheers*, *Taxi*, *Hill Street Blues* and *ER* that extends into more recent entertainment vehicles in work settings such as *The West Wing*, *The Office*, and *Grey's Anatomy*.

The popularity and endurance of these shows coincided with other important societal trends that began during this era. Social observers such as Robert Putnam have noted a gradual erosion of social capital, that is, the networks of social relationships characterized by norms of reciprocity and trustworthiness that form the fabric of communal activity beginning in this time period. Due to such factors as increased mobility and suburban sprawl, television, and increased pressures of time and money, people became less connected to well-established social structures such as civic organizations and deeply rooted neighborhoods.[1] It seemed that workplaces were beginning to fill this emotional void, and provide more opportunities for these social bonds, and perhaps these work-based shows reflected a deeper desire to develop more deep social connections in office environments and, in the fashion of *Cheers*, to have "a place where everybody knows your name." The trends continued in the 1980s and 1990s as teams, quality circles, and a growing emphasis on "empowerment" in relationships and human interaction. As I often tell my students, people bring their humanity to work and, although they may appropriately downplay their personal lives, they do not check their emotions at the door. It is possible and perhaps even desirable to form meaningful relationships that often grow into friendships while the work is getting done. Putnam cautions, however, that some recent trends such as downsizing in the face of global competition and a sluggish economy have made work more contingent, undermining the implicit employment contract and may weaken these important social ties at work.

Despite these misgivings, workplaces can set the stage for the emergence of powerful relationships. Consider, for example, the current real version of *The West Wing*, the Obama White House, and the special mentor relationship between the President's chief advisor, David Axelrod, and his young special assistant, Eric Lesser.[2] This organizational odd couple has been depicted as a latter day "Oscar and Felix" with the younger more organized and fastidious assistant keeping the older, professorial and "non-linear" thinking boss in line and on schedule. There is a comedic interplay between these two characters that belies a deep caring and appreciation of one another. It also fits the mentor–protégé relationship described in the previous chapter. Such pairings are very common in organizational life and can be found in much less visible and famous settings.

James Krantz refers to these pairings as "managerial couples" that:

> can take on a life of their own, replete with shared fantasies, hopes and disappointments, collaborative dialogue, and collusive defensive patterns. On one end of a continuum is the productive, creative, evolving, and mutually stimulating couple. On the other is the rigid, stalemated, sometimes mutually punishing relationship characterized by excessive conflict, numbing detachment, or debilitating dependency.[3]

It was clear in this manager study that the best managers were those who built and nurtured relationships that enabled them to be mentors and teachers who were open, supportive, and trustworthy in the eyes of their employees. As one respondent commented:

> In my experience the best managers I have worked with so far in my career, are able to establish a mutually beneficial relationship with their employees. More specifically I know that I am much more eager to work as hard as possible for a manager who verbally expresses their appreciation for my hard work. This type of manager is able to influence, instruct and inspire all while respecting and being appreciative of their employees' work.

It was striking how personal many of the 1,058 responses documented in Chapter 2 were with predominant themes such as *respect* (mentioned in 144 cases), *trust* (132 cases), and *good communication* (104 cases) in the descriptions of best managers. The term "relationship" was specifically mentioned in 49 best manager cases. Very few people when speaking of best managers referred primarily to their technical ability, such as their prowess with enterprise software or their deep knowledge of financial markets. It is not because these factors were unimportant. After all, business knowledge and acumen are essential elements for effective performance and there were several comments about how well these managers knew their business. But, just as we have seen that left brain functions and IQ interact with more right brain EQ factors, with these respondents the personal and the professional aspects were inextricably linked. They were concerned about how the manager built a *supportive environment* (198 cases), how well they *listened* (112 cases), and how well they gave *feedback* (97 cases). Several of the same interpersonal issues showed up in stories about the worst managers in their opposite form: *poor communication* (104 cases), *disrespect* (89 cases), *lack of trust* (70 cases), *lack of feedback* (56 cases), and *poor listening* (46 cases). Interestingly, even with worst managers, the word "incompetent" was used in only 12 cases. Each of these themes will be addressed in greater detail along with specific case examples that reveal the depth and complexity of these relationships.

A Matter of Trust

Thus wrote Billy Joel in his rock and roll meditation on love and relationships. Trust is perhaps the most fundamental building block of all relationships. Erik Erikson proclaimed a sense of basic trust, that is, trusting of others and oneself, as the fundamental prerequisite of mental vitality reaching back to infancy.[4] A *good enough mother* (and similarly a *good enough manager*) through daily interactions creates and reinforces this cornerstone of effective relationships. It is no surprise that when I ask students or executives to list the qualities of a good working relationship, trust emerges as one of the first qualities along with mutual respect and honesty. As the management scholar Manfred Kets de Vries concluded: "trust is a very delicate flower – one that takes a long time to blossom and is easily crushed."[5]

There were numerous cases and stories where trust was the predominant theme. Here is one definition that combines several interconnected elements:

> I have never had a perfect manager. I have had some very good managers and it is hard to pick one as the best. I've had very good female and male managers, but I've had more female managers. The things I think are important include (being) respectful of people's talents, mutual trust, those that will stop and listen, those that will go to bat for you so you will be recognized, those that will allow you to grow without letting you hang out to dry, those that have courage to fight for their associates.

Trust here is seen in a very developmental way. It is important that workers feel like someone is looking out for their best interests and will not "hang them out to dry." Instead, employees can experience the possibility of growing as part of their job and being recognized for their efforts.

The "good enough" theme again emerges in the following scenario as the manager is described as creating the facilitating environment, displaying the trust necessary for autonomous behavior to emerge within well-managed boundaries:

> My manager was VERY trusting. Upon starting in the position, there was an underlying assumption and trust that I could handle the job and all the responsibilities that came along with it. It helped me to have confidence in myself. It was kind of a "sink or swim" environment. I was given my responsibilities and just allowed to run with them ... even though this was an entry-level, post MBA position. I appreciated the flexibility to think outside of the box, which was always rewarded. My manager would always ask my opinion on the vision and strategy the department should take. She genuinely respected and valued my input. My manager was likeable. She was friendly and showed a genuine, friendly interest in what was going on in my life. We became friends, yet she never crossed the professional boundary. Without my asking, she would just provide guidance and advice without seeming parental or over bearing. She could somehow give me critical feedback on my performance and leave me feeling grateful for the advice and excited on trying again next time. It was a true art.

The reference to managing as an art is noteworthy. It is reminiscent of Anne Morrow Lindbergh's dancers, "barely touching as they pass, but partners in the same pattern," presented in Chapter 1. The relationship is personal ... but not too personal, parental but not overbearing. The GEM has to trust enough to let go so that individual performance can flourish, as in the following case where an employee's admitted tendency toward perfectionism is moderated by a manager's broader perspective:

> My best manager is one that instilled trust and achieved this through frank and open communication. He saw the best intentions of people long before assuming their worst. He genuinely managed people like he himself wanted to be managed. I am a project manager and tend to be very critical of myself and the success of my assigned projects. I've suffered from "perfectionism" and I am judgmental when things don't work to their most optimum outcome. I remember a time when I had a string of "less than successful" projects. This very good manager would review my performance and would point out where things may have gone wrong, but he went further. He provided a broader view and pointed out positive results that I wasn't aware of. For example, I was

quite rejected after returning from a steering committee meeting after freezing one of my projects. But he pointed out that this company had a history of leaving stagnant projects open. They would remain open and continue to collect costs and charges even though no progress was ever achieved. And by pushing to freeze this project, I helped to close it off the books and this would help to focus the organization on the remainder of the portfolio. I'm not sure I ever really "bought" into this particular rationalization, but it made me feel better. And I think it is a good example of open conversation, assuming the best of intentions, and seeing the bigger picture.

So how is this kind of trustworthy managing actually done? Is there a model to follow? The following tale provides a set of working guidelines for a manager, particularly when an employee needs to be confronted for stepping out of line:

> Several years ago I worked for someone who would clearly fall into the "best" category. In no particular order: Employee Development – this manager took the time to get to know me and my work style; she then adjusted her approach to build on my strengths while also providing me the opportunity to work with things I was less familiar with. For example, when giving me a new project, she would first ensure that the pieces she wanted to discuss with me were in place (she actually made a point of stating this to me as well). As she came to realize my abilities in analysis, attention to detail, and picking things up quickly, she helped build my confidence by not only turning the responsibility for the project over to me, but also acknowledging my input in subtle ways ("As you pointed out..." or "You made a good point when..."). In addition, she kept track of a great number of the smaller items I had worked on throughout the year and mentioned all of them on my performance review. For those tasks I was not so familiar with, she was very approachable and answered my questions directly without talking in circles or re-explaining the entire concept and still not answering the question (see "worst manager – 1st runner up" for that one). Professionalism – this manager was very intelligent and personable, and had a great sense of humor. Yet even though it was very easy to talk to her, there was never any doubt that we were there to get a job done. She was organized, gave reasonable deadlines, helped you meet them if need be, but she held you to them and always met them herself. Respectful – this manager gave corrective feedback in a very professional, productive manner. An example: one day when she expected me to be working on something, it seemed as though every time she came over to my desk I was writing an email (coincidence – honest!) Actually, the emails had to do with trying

to find a new place to live as my marriage was breaking up – and the information just couldn't wait. She called me into her office and mentioned the work I had to do in a calm, non-accusatory tone. I think she also asked if there was a problem and if we needed to discuss it. I indicated there was an issue, but said I'd rather not discuss it, and then I thanked her for bringing the email issue to my attention and went back to work. This episode made a huge impression on me because I felt as though she treated me with respect. Confrontation to correct someone is really difficult and there are a lot of managers who will avoid it – but then carry a grudge because they're annoyed at you. She knew me well enough to know I wasn't a slacker – so she didn't jump to that erroneous conclusion – but I've seen such things happen and it seems as though once the manager forms such an "opinion," the employee can no longer do anything right in the manager's eyes. I have a lot of respect for the way she handled this situation. Career Development/Not Threatened by my Success – this manager shared stories of her professional experiences with me and offered helpful advice on professional education and the workings of corporate America. She even encouraged me to get more "face time" with higher-level managers and made sure these people knew my achievements and abilities. Not only would she never have taken credit for my work, but instead she made a point of letting higher-ups know when I did something particularly well. She had my trust as well as my appreciation; it was a great experience to work for her.

It is particularly noteworthy that this series of experiences resulted in building "trust and appreciation" on the part of this employee. The manager was very straightforward, gave specific feedback, and kept the issue that needed correcting in proper perspective. The manager respected the employee's personal boundaries while still getting the message across. She focused on the behavior and what needed to be done and continued to develop this employee.

It is often said that "trust begets trust" and is contagious, as the following example illustrates:

He was a good manager for me for a lot reasons but mostly because I felt trusted and this was important to me. I also had a team of 4 people reporting to me. When your boss trusts you the positive implications are enormous for an organization because I believe this leads you to perform a better job, to project this trust to the rest of the team. It helps to unify different parts of an organization. If my boss trusts me, and I trust my people, my people trust my boss. Everybody is happy. He was honest and opened himself and talked about his experiences. By doing this I learned what things were important for him. This helped me to manage our information flow better. It is important to know what your boss needs/wants so he can be kept informed about it. Ongoing communication – even if might seem minor – is important. Certain types of reporting needs to be established beforehand, but in the real world you also need to report day to day issues, problems ... that are not in a list. Learning what to report is crucial but your boss needs to open himself for you to understand him better and know what he might consider an "important matter." He knew how to delegate. He was extremely respectful and had a great sense of humor. My department was extremely technical and he was not technical at all but he always showed interest to broadly understand the technicality of our projects. (He was) always willing to listen. He was very diplomatic with sensitive issues. And he NEVER LOST HIS TEMPER.

Once again we see how managing emotions and appropriately using humor can have a powerful effect. Trust moves from one person to the other, eventually embracing the entire organization. By opening himself up to his employees, this manager enabled his employees to better know his needs and what he considers important, so that they can manage up and even educate the boss in areas (such as technology) that may not be one of his strengths. Everyone benefits.

The View from Under the Bus

Once again, a lot can be learned about a phenomenon by viewing its opposite. Stories about worst manager experiences often made the link between the dominant theme of "micro-managing" and lack of trust. Here is one about a boss who just could not let go:

> My worst manager was someone that could not let projects go. I would be "in charge" of a project but she would micromanage the entire thing. Sometimes, I would start working on something that was due in a week and she would already have started working on it as well but without telling me. So we would do double the work. She was not comfortable with trusting people to do their jobs.

An old saying states that if you want something done right, do it yourself, but it does not always apply when you are in a leadership role. It may help to avoid confronting an uncomfortable conversation with a lackluster employee, but the micro-managing sends the implicit message to other hard-working employees that the manager does not trust them to do their own work. It can also create more stress, as the micro-managing boss takes on more and more to the detriment of all.

On the other hand, the following example focuses on a lack of definition or boundaries at the beginning, leading to fear and insecurity with lingering impact:

> My worst manager was one that kept me in fear of my job. She was after me from the start and did not give me the direction or tools to correct myself in order to better fit with the organization. It wasn't a need to have my hand held – but rather a need to know what would be required and what steps to succeed and meet expectations. No direction, no definition of expectations. Direct conversation on the topic would lead to nothing for answers. I never knew where I stood and lived in constant fear of failure and the consequences of failure. The effect was dramatic. A normally self confident individual, I was reduced to fear, physical discomfort, and even stammering in front of this individual and hence my performance was a self fulfilling prophecy. It instilled a sense of distrust in managers that I still battle with 17 years later.

Seventeen years is a long time to feel the ripple effects of a manager who induced both fear and distrust. Here, there were no "guardrails" and the resulting anxiety is obvious and debilitating in a variety of ways. It is most interesting to note that this employee did not need "hand-holding," but rather a good enough "holding environment" where boundaries and expectations are clearly and consistently communicated. The next instance from the world of accounting reveals how inconsistency, alternatively micro-managing and letting go at the wrong times, leads to a breakdown in trust:

> My worst manager made me feel the exact opposite of my best manager – not valued and untrustworthy. This manager would micro-manage me in areas where I did not need help and would not help me in areas where I was seeking guidance. Example – I am a CPA (and) he is a CFA. He would often question my interpretation of GAAP (Generally Accepted Accounting Principles) and require I get other CPAs in the company to verify my work. However, when I sought his help on developing a financial model for analyzing derivative instruments (something I had little experience with and he had a lot) he told me to "figure it out." I was later reprimanded for doing the work incorrectly. He also loved the spotlight and would take all the credit for high profile projects and leave me with the grunt work. He once reprimanded me for speaking to his boss (the Corporate Treasurer) without telling him first even though the topic was not an area of his responsibility or expertise. He often would give me tasks to do without providing any insight as to what objective

the task related to, making it difficult to complete the task correctly and then would complain when the work was not done as expected. He would never tell me what was going on within the department which always made me feel like I could not be trusted. He often would go to off-site meetings or trainings for days and not tell me that he was going to be out of the office. I usually found out from others (outside of my department) where he was and what he was doing. The only feedback I received was when I did something wrong. I went into my performance review expecting a bad review and was shocked when I received a glowing one. I was lucky to be offered a job in another department so I could get away from this manager. The two individuals who took on my role after me both quit within six months of taking the job, citing the inability to work for or with this manager.

In several instances, even the so-called worst managers were described as technically competent with strong work ethics, but just couldn't manage either themselves or their people, creating an environment that was distrustful and, at times, even hostile.

My worst manager was a man who had fantastic ideas but could never organize his company and keep everything straight. And he didn't have the trust/intelligence/foresight to allow someone else to do it for him. For example he would sit in meetings (and this occurred multiple times a week) and come up with brilliant ideas on where to take the company. But none of it would ever get done, because he never allowed anyone to start the ball rolling. He would just come up with new ideas the next day and go all "control freak" on that idea. Our small group of interns that summer gave up caring after a few weeks because we knew he would send us in a new direction the next day, and would never trust any of us with carrying the reins on one of his projects.

I've had two prior male managers that were classic "type A" leaders in that they were in well-deserved positions of power based on their track records and work-related competencies, but they always seemed to be a bit socially inept: always defensive, stirring the pot with people, and heightening their own and others' sense of paranoia/self consciousness. The impact of these personalities always made for a weird team dynamic (one that always lacked trust!). These managers engaged in ongoing teasing/joking/etc. of people around them in a way that made people uncomfortable (they would talk about people behind their backs, make jokes at the expense of others, and call people out in meetings). I think people never felt relaxed around them. When given the opportunity, you felt like they would "throw you under the bus" as their employee (and they might have, unbeknownst to you). In addition, one thing I noticed about these managers was that they always seemed to be testing/ pushing the limits of "sexual harassment". They were always "joking" with people to see how comfortable/cool they handled the situations they put you in (i.e. if you let them say inappropriate things around you, you were considered "cool" or "in the inner circle"). Maybe they weren't even "testing" these people and this is just who they were and they couldn't "turn it off" at work. Any matter, I'd classify these managers as socially immature and extremely self-absorbed. Looking back, I felt like I worked way too hard to "impress" these managers and make them happy in order to remain on their good side (instead of feeling like they were working hard for me as their employee). This is very different than the situation that I'm in now where I feel like my manager and I have mutual respect for each other. Now that I'm in a different work situation (i.e. with a good manager at a different company), I don't go home thinking about/dwelling on/stressing about my manager anymore during my free time. I'm glad I had those experiences from a learning standpoint, but from a quality of life standpoint, I'm happy to be out of there!

Call them brilliant "control freaks" or "Type As," or worse, it appears that these managers rose to their positions based on their cognitive intelligence and bright ideas. Yet, they either could not let others put their brilliant ideas into action or they engaged in socially immature and narcissistic behavior that rendered others paranoid and distrustful. This kind of managerial style leads to the "false self" as employees bend over backwards and work too hard to please and stay on their good side. Although employees can learn from these managerial experiences, they look better in the rear-view mirror.

Mutual Respect

Like lightning and thunder, trust and respect are closely linked and were often spoken of in the same response. Once a sense of trust is experienced, respect tends to follow. Those who study human relationships cite "mutualism" and "reciprocal altruism" as behaviors that have evolved over eons to serve as the basis for relationships within and among families, friends, and communities ... including work communities.[6] Trust and mutual respect are essential for good working relationships and create the foundation for effective interactions, and even negotiations, which can take on a more adversarial stance. As Roger Fisher and William Ury state, "A working relationship where trust, understanding, respect, and friendship are built up over time can make each new negotiation smoother and more efficient."[7] The key is that these relationships take time to develop and grow.

Such an evolving mutual relationship is visually depicted in the famous image *Drawing Hands* by the artist M.C. Escher (see Figure 4.1). Each hand is both separate and connected in a never-ending mutual cycle where each is simultaneously drawing and being drawn by the other.[8] It is hard to tell which hand is the dominant one, as both are mutually influencing each other. Many relationships ultimately become power struggles, where each person seeks to gain "the upper hand," so to speak.

The image reinforces the idea that relationships are never stagnant and are constantly evolving. The hands are in a continuous state of being created and elaborated and thus are never complete or perfected. Respect is one of those qualities that tend to be returned if given. Most cultures and religions have some version of the Golden Rule: *do unto others as you would have them do unto you*. A good enough manager puts this into practice through respectful behavior and a genuine appreciation of the other as a separate, yet connected, human being.

In the cases where respect was specifically mentioned, it was usually in the context of other factors such as trust and the mentor-teaching relationship discussed earlier. Respondents referred to mutual respect, a manager's respect for employees' expertise, ideas, and time, and respectful or courteous behavior. Consider the following two examples:

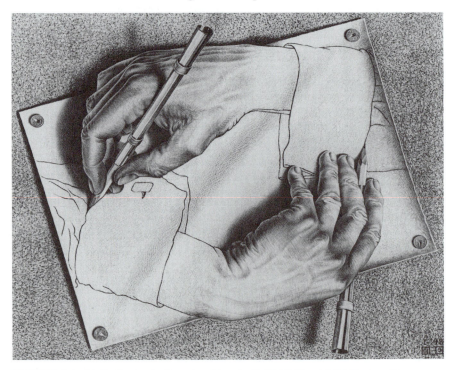

FIGURE 4.1. M.C. Escher's *Drawing Hands* © 2010 The M.C. Escher Company-Holland. All rights reserved.

The best manager I ever had was someone who took the time to really get to know me. He was someone who would stick up for his direct reports when the situation warranted it. He had a genuinely caring nature that not only prompted mutual respect, but also drove me to work as hard as I could to make him proud of me.

This person demonstrated a genuine interest in me as a person, as well as a professional. He made extra effort to involve me in learning opportunities and was both direct and truthful with me. He offered constructive criticism and supported me as I learned from my mistakes. He treats everyone he encounters with respect and has earned the respect of virtually every member of his staff, as well as those he interacts with. Being someone very senior in the organization, he embraces the "open door" policy and treats staff of all levels in a fair and respectful manner.

In each of these cases, the word "genuine" appears along with respect. These managers take the time to get to know their employees at a deeper level and show caring and concern for the person and their performance in their role. The respect is given, and returned in the form of hard work and a desire to "make him proud." Likewise the following more generic description highlights in more detail how such a manager demonstrates respect:

The best manager is someone who shows respect to his/her employees (private discussions, no yelling, empathetic, sympathetic, shows compassion where necessary, understands the employee has a life outside the office/building/company). The best manager is someone who can "see" or "hear" things others can't (for example, a troubled employees shows signs like depression, unhappiness, even excitement, anxiety). The best manager would be able to recognize these and "delve" a little into them in order to help employees (decisions: do they need EAP? Can something at work change to accommodate like hours? Is it someone within the group/office/company causing this issue? Can human resources help? Does this person need to take time away? Does the compensation package allow for this person to take time away and not lose pay?) The best manager also knows, can CLEARLY explain and lay out, understand, encourage and reward their employees work towards accomplishing the business practices, and the company's goals, targets, etc. The best manager is a manager whose employees enjoy working for. Someone they respect and want to work with everyday. Someone they will miss if he/she left the company.

The next examples focus on more specific situations where respect was the primary theme:

I have worked for two "BEST" managers. Each treated their associates with respect, both for the associate as an individual and as a "person" who had a life outside the 9–5 workplace. My first son was born premature and required frequent hospitalizations when he was an infant. This required me to take time off from work, sometimes without notice. My boss was completely supportive of me during this time, saying that, "When you are here, you give me 110% percent – and you always have. The least I can do is support you while you're going through this with your son." My second "best" boss charged me with creating a new team dedicated to analyzing the effectiveness of the company's quality control procedures. He also treated people with dignity and respect. He understood that I have a passion for creating something new and gave me a lot of freedom and independence to build this new team, instead of micromanaging the process. He showed not only that he respected my ability to build the team, but he also showed his trust in me that I would do the job.

The first "best" manager recognized that some life situations transcend work and, in effect said, "You work hard for me, so I will support you during this crisis." It is noteworthy in the last example the respect for the employee's ability is linked to the capacity to allow that employee to run with a creative passion, connecting respect with the "good enough" theme of autonomy and not micro-managing.

By contrast, respondents were more than eager to share stories of disrespectful managers or those that commanded little respect for their employees and colleagues. One was quite succinct: "He was the worst manager because he was dishonest, disrespectful, lazy, insecure and abusive." Others wrote of managers who were emotionally volatile, or arrogant, leaving lots of damage in their wake:

My worst boss was very abrasive and self-righteous. If she didn't agree with someone or something she would disrupt the meeting and make her point. She generally would start yelling at a meeting and become very argumentative which was very disrespectful to colleagues and vendors. The worst was when a work group requested her removal from the project and I replaced her as a project manager. After I started managing the project, I set up a meeting to demonstrate the capabilities of a new software (application) and she disrupted the entire meeting with questions, instead of asking me questions off-line. These type of situations happened with other departments and I would be asked about her erratic behaviors. It was a very uncomfortable situation for me as a subordinate. Ultimately, she was lacking interpersonal communication skills as well as self-control.

My worst manager was quite arrogant and acted as if he knew every-thing. Many times when asking questions it was evident he would give answers simply to have a response and was as unclear about what I was asking as I was. It led to a great lack of trust and respect and the need to go over his head in order to receive proper guidance and answers. At the times he did know the answers to questions and he explained them as if I were a child, showing a complete lack of respect for a fellow co-worker.

Such an easy one ... This manager actually told me that I "cared too much" about the five people who I managed. She was the most insensi-tive, scattered, heartless, person I have ever come in contact with. She would be your friend at one moment and your worst enemy the next. She had NO respect for anyone who worked for her. None of the people who worked for (her) ever felt like we were an asset to her team. She was the reason I left that company. Many people left before me and after me because of this manager.

Other managers were consummate game-players, often engaging in destruc-tive politics, withholding information for their personal gain, or pitting one employee against another:

This person fails in virtually every respect of managing people. He demands respect, believing his title precludes him from needing to earn it (he actually said this to me). He does not treat his staff with respect and does not stand behind them publicly. He has an aversion to confron-tation and is therefore unable to offer direct feedback (constructive or otherwise) and instead talks behind people's backs. The result is that employees seldom know where they truly stand with him. He uses the word "I" extensively, specifically in circumstances where a skilled leader would say "We." His personal insecurities dictate much of his profes-sional behavior, and as a result, he is unable to collaborate on inter-department initiatives. Rather, he constantly identifies ways to position himself against other members of a team. As a result, most of his projects fall behind schedule and result in the messy politics of finger-pointing.

The worst manager tried to create fierce competition between me and a peer. This person thought that they could get great results by creating a cut-throat culture of competition where we would always try to one-up each other. This manager played both sides and told us both we were in line for her job and that she supported us. It created an unhealthy envir-onment where my peer left and I lost all respect for the manager. She was eventually fired.

The worst manager does not share information or communicate well with the team, leading to gaps in knowledge and not being able to provide our business partners with superior service and partnerships; does not allow us as a team to grow together, but rather keeps us guessing and having to pull pieces of the puzzle together to ensure that we have all the information before moving to action; talks about others in a negative way, leading to mistrust and a lack of respect. (If she talks about others this way, then what is she saying about me?); does not take ownership – pushes ownership off of her and does not help to be a part of the solution, but is part of the problem (i.e. by her lack of communication); does not listen so that she can help to build solutions with me or the team and take ownership for things. An example – I raised a critical issue to her about a concern that I had with a business partner. I felt that I had done all that I could to address the issue, including several different communication approaches, etc. I engaged my manager to help me perhaps determine another approach or solution to alleviate my concern. Her response was "well, you've done all that you can do and at least you have covered yourself because you have it in writing." This was not the response that I was looking for from a very senior person in the organization. At her level, my expectation for support was very different from her response to me.

This last example illustrates how an atmosphere of distrust and disrespect combine with the manager's failure to engage with an employee needing help with a problem situation. The manager seemed more concerned about making sure this employee had "covered" himself rather than directly addressing the issue. A good enough manager senses when to step in and when to trust the employee to work it out for himself.

Closely tied to disrespect was behavior that I have encapsulated under the banner of "condescending" that includes demeaning, humiliating, demoralizing, and at times, just plain bullying:

Probably the "worst of the worst": despicable, tyrannical, dogmatic, disrespectful, prejudiced, cunning, cheating, hurtful, degrading, demeaning, callous, manipulative. This person in contrast was my worst experience. He made promises he did not keep, cheated me and others out of overtime and was audited by the Feds eventually, spoke down to employees, swore, humiliated the female workers, violated employment laws, cheated and misrepresented to customers. People feared him and he preyed on those that really needed the job, he knew I could walk away and he left me alone but I still felt the negativity he generated. It was so bad customers could feel the negativity when they walked into the store.

The worst manager I ever worked for was my first one. He managed by fear and intimidation. You were either one of his favored or you were not. He routinely left people in tears. He was highly egotistical and had very little, if any, empathy for others. He viewed and spoke about his peers with open scorn. He seemed to delight in using his power over others, being confrontational and belittling and intimidating people. Our company had recently gone through a merger and those who weren't laid off were shuffled around to different jobs and divisions. My old boss moved over to my then new husband's division although they were in different product areas. Right after returning from my honeymoon, I attended a meeting with about 20 people including my old boss (who I no longer worked for). As the meeting was adjourning, he stood up and told me in front of the rest of the attendants that my husband (who worked in a different division than either of us) had just been laid off and likely had been escorted out of the building (this is a common business practice in the financial industry). He had no business making this announcement – period, other than to be spiteful.

The worst manager ever … many of us that have interacted with her believe her to be mentally ill. Her style was to pick on one person at a time on the team. After going through two or three others on the team over the course of two to three months, I became her whipping post. She would say she was always available to meet, but actually wouldn't keep her one-on-one meeting times. As a result, I was often in the situation of presenting at a meeting without having the chance to run my presentation by her first. She attacked me repeatedly in team meetings, meetings with other departments, and meetings with vendors. Imagine trying to be effective in a company after having been yelled at (literally with loud voice) in front of peers, subordinates, and executives. It was miserable. I was looking for a new job the entire time. Finally, she left the company. I was validated when she was fired after only five months at her next VP level job. I needed to read some books on the subject and talk to other people that knew her from previous jobs to get back my self-confidence. Reading her profile in a book that labeled her behavior as a "bully" really helped. Also, learning how to deal with her type has helped. That situation will never happen to me again. It was horrible!!!!

Managed by intimidation, negative criticism and yelling. Created a negative work environment with significant personnel turnover. No social interactions. Had the opinion that if you didn't like it (the workplace) then get out. One story sticks in my mind. The industry was a mortgage company, new to the northeast area of the country. Over the first half of the year the office processed, closed and sold off the most mortgage loans of any other office in the country. She comes into work and calls a meeting to tell everyone what the office has accomplished. Then she announces she's off to get her nails done so she'll look great when the district manager comes later that day to take her out to dinner and go over the bonus money she's earned. The staff who processed the work got nothing; not even pizza for lunch. Unbelievably the worst manager I've ever worked for. She reminds me of Cruella DeVille. Mean to the core.

While my "worst" boss was actually a pretty decent peer, once the organization changed and I started reporting into him, I realized what a bad manager he is. He is a brilliant technologist, but has no understanding of people or any regard for anything but his own ambition. He does not communicate with his team, he does not give clear direction, and he is demeaning to individuals "below" him. He only manages up – not across or down. I have many stories whirling through my head, but here's an overall summary. Through great changes in the organization, he was promoted to a senior executive level and continues to move various organizations under him even though he has no background, no time to devote to these teams, and has actually said he is building his resume. He is disliked by the entire organization, and he is actually one of the primary reasons I am leaving the company after ten years.

It is worth noting that this constellation of negative behaviors, often stereotypically attributed to males, was evenly distributed across males and females. What underlies this behavior? Laura Crawshaw, an executive coach and self-described "boss whisperer" defines an "abrasive" boss as one who rubs co-workers the wrong way through aggressive behavior that inflicts lasting wounds to the point of disrupting organizational functioning.[9] These bosses seem hell-bent on preserving their dominant status and are personally threatened by what they perceive as "incompetence." They believe in intimidating co-workers into their version of competence. On the other hand *good enough managers* do not see this kind of perceived incompetence as a personal threat; rather, they see it as a problem to be solved. They assess the situation as objectively as possible and then adapt accordingly.

Clear and Responsive Communicators

We live in a time of unparalleled capacity to communicate. Innovations in information technology have enabled us to get our message to *anyone anytime and anywhere* with the click of a mouse or the stroke of a thumb on a keypad.

Instant messaging and texting have supplanted email as a way to get a message across quickly and efficiently. In the last few years, social media such as Facebook and Twitter have greatly expanded our horizons as the desire to connect and be part of a continuous information flow has exponentially grown. The overarching feature of these relatively new electronic communication forms is the sharing of information – actually the sharing of one's "self," or a constructed version of oneself – with concentric circles of contacts and connections. There has been a fundamental shift from private to public as individuals share ideas, observations, life status updates, and pictures with either a chosen few or the whole world.

The next generation of employees has been labeled "Generation C": connected, communicating, content-centric, computerized, community-oriented, and constantly clicking. They came of age during the 2000s and by the year 2020 will make up 40 percent of the population of the United States, Europe, and the BRIC countries (Brazil, Russia, India, and China). They have never known life without the Internet, mobile devices and social networking, and spend as much as six hours a day using these devices, staying in contact with large networks of family, friends, people with common interests, and business contacts. They are already having a profound effect on the business world. According to a Booz & Company survey, employees will bring their personal computers to work and rely less on corporate information technology, organizations will become increasingly virtual, global, and less hierarchical, and workers will seamlessly mix personal and professional aspects of their lives.[10]

Communication scholars as well as social scientists will uncover new meaning in these evolving forms. For example, Sherry Turkle at MIT's Initiative on Technology and Self raises a concern about the fact that teens that spend increasing amounts of time texting, meaning less time in face-to-face communication, thus slowing their emotional growth, trading real intimacy for the illusion of companionship.[11] Writing about the growing prominence of social networking, Malcolm Gladwell observes that social media are built upon a platform of "weak ties" that enable people to organize and follow a large group of acquaintances. These weaker social ties, however, are often our main source for new information, providing ready access to innovation and interdisciplinary collaboration.[12] Gladwell posits that strategic thinking requires the discipline of hierarchies, or, as he puts it, the social networks are great for organizing suppliers and customers, but not necessarily for establishing a coherent design philosophy for products such as cars. This is why social media, characterized by widely dispersed and consensus-based networks, are proving helpful as a way to disseminate information throughout and among organizations. The ability to enhance communication with uploaded video clips and live feeds, playable on a multitude of devices, has enabled the inclusion and "liberation" of more nonverbal language in addition to verbal, increasing the meaning and more closely approximating a live experience.[13] Twitter and Facebook are now essential marketing tools as consumers are invited to follow their favorite products, celebrities, and politicians, creating an immediacy of interactive experience. We also have witnessed how powerful social media have been in fueling the political uprisings, particularly among young people, in Middle Eastern countries such as Tunisia and Egypt with profound impact.

Still, there is something bemusing about reading the random postings of the highlights of a person's daily existence ("I'm having soup!"). At times, they seem to reveal a certain urgency in the desire to make themselves visible and known ... as if to see if anyone in an increasingly fragmented and impersonal world notices. And notice they often do because someone will react ("I love soup!"), or, if it is Facebook, three people will indicate that they "like" whatever news item was posted. It's fun and can sometimes serve to develop new relationships or reinforce existing ones. However, for all of the potential of these pervasive communication vehicles, there is a possible downside. It was actually Winnicott who posed the idea that "the capacity to be alone" is a foundation for emotional health and a prerequisite for building good relationships.[14] Some social observers wonder if this crucial capacity – the ability to reflect and to be with one's own thoughts – is diminishing in this hyper-connected world and that the only way a person can experience a sense of self, or to render an opinion or decision, is to send a message. It is almost as if the communicator is saying to someone, anyone, "I exist." "I tweet, therefore I am."[15]

The organizational world, in particular the business and professional domains, is not usually known for clarity of communication. All professions have their unique language conventions and word usages that help define the culture. As with any culture, if you know the language, you gain ready access. Thus we have managers showing their creativity by "thinking outside the box" to come up with "value-added solutions" to maintain a "customer-friendly" environment. They change nouns to verbs to indicate "forward thinking" action in order to "incent" their employees to "utilize their knowledge capital to achieve competitive advantage." They also "leverage" a lot of things: money, people, and ideas. They employ sports or military metaphors to "move the ball down the field" and "blow them out of the water." The late comedian and social critic George Carlin noted the inflation inherent in business language where clerks become "associates" or "sales representatives," secretaries become "personal or executive assistants" (except, of course for the Secretary of State and other Cabinet officers) and retail store security people are now "loss prevention managers." It sounds better ... or does it? Likewise, employees who lose their jobs for performance or economic reasons are "right-sized," "re-engineered," "deselected," or part of a "focused reduction."[16] Such euphemisms seem designed to bend or soften the harsh reality of losing a job. Perhaps it is well intended to ease negative emotions or to bolster self-esteem associated with mundane work. The unfortunate effect is often the creation of a false reality that increases cynicism and erodes trust in those who employ this kind of non-communication.

What we learn from the above communication observations and challenges is that with so many alternatives available, making the proper choice of the best means (do I call, text, send an actual handwritten note, or sit down over coffee and talk this one out face-to-face?), and using the right words at the right time with the proper and intended emotional tone, becomes an increasingly rare and much appreciated phenomenon. It is no wonder that the best managers in the study were seen as excellent communicators. Their talent at communicating was most often seen within the context of being a good enough mentor or teacher, or creating a trusting and respectful environment as shown by these examples:

> The best manager with whom I've ever worked possessed three critical skills. 1. Outstanding communicator: not just verbal (obvious); non-verbal was just as important if not more so, as it was the guiding force behind his words; the last piece was simply the realization that the more he communicated with his team, by keeping them "in the know," the more success he attained through our actions and innovations. 2. Recognized Strengths/Weaknesses: He realized where we excelled and failed as team members and then put us each in the best position to succeed. More importantly, he focused training and mentoring on those weaknesses so we would be better equipped in the future. 3. Adapted well: Changed his management style to the person, the level, and the audience. This generated great success.

> The individual is the "best manager" because he is always willing to take the time to ensure that I have an understanding of the issue that I am working on. The manager explains through the use of examples, and also encourages me to stop him at any point, whether I don't understand the material or to stop him because I am already familiar with what he is showing me. He is also understanding of my personal life, though he asks a lot from me (work late hours and weekends), he understands when I have an appointment or a family commitment, and we work around them.

> My best manager was an incredible motivator. He inspired us to perform at our best and always expected the highest standards. He often gave us assignments that challenged our own expectations of ourselves. For example, when he went on vacation or was out of town he would appoint one of his direct reports as his "stand in" while he was away. He really

meant business on that. We knew we could be called upon at any time to make higher level decisions than we were accustomed to. He also gave frequent feedback, never hesitating to walk into my office to pass along a compliment on my work that had been delivered to him verbally or in writing. This individual also delegated work completely, giving us full responsibility for a task. We knew we would get full credit if we succeeded. However, if we made a mistake and messed up he would help us get out of any jam. This manager gave frequent awards and acknowledgements. He recognized his best performers in front of his entire division, and did not distinguish between VPs (of which I was one) and clerical level people. All were worthy of public praise. We used to joke about it, because he was always coming up with a new name to an award. But we appreciated receiving them and appreciated when he would let us give them out, too. He was confident both personally and professionally and rarely got mired in office politics. He would tell us that our job was to develop our successor, something that some professionals are scared to do. It is threatening to know that someone who reports to you is being groomed to do your job, but that's what he wanted us to do. He always wanted the ability to pull us out of our job and into something bigger, and he needed to know that we had an eye on one of our direct reports to become our replacement. He often changed or rotated our assignments so we couldn't get bored. He had lots of good advice on communication. Some of his sayings are stuck in my mind 10 years later. One of them is "The only problem with communication is the illusion that it has taken place." This comes to mind often.

The value of effective communication was also made evident when it was lacking, as the following examples illustrate:

About eight years into my career, I was working as the senior financial person in a venture capital firm. The time had come for the firm to hire a CFO that I would report to. Our first interaction was a full morning meeting where he reviewed everything I did in the firm. Our next one was the day he told me what aspects of my job he was going to take over and what ones I would keep. He was a terrible communicator. I would find out things after they happened and would usually also find out that I was responsible for them after the fact. He was never able to clearly delineate where my job ended and his began. When I decided to change jobs and after submitting my letter of resignation, he asked me to see him for an exit interview. He accused me of "working with the enemy" (I was joining a competitor) amongst other things without even giving me a chance to explain what the circumstances were. Because the conversation was one-sided, I walked out of his office, packed my things and never returned. This was a person who failed to demonstrate a willingness to work with me, to delineate responsibilities, to effectively communicate things as they were occurring rather than after they occurred and didn't take the time to understand or give a person the opportunity to explain situations before acting on them.

Individual is inaccessible, fails to prioritize, never communicates and when you elevate an issue you don't get support. The only time you hear from this manager is when something goes wrong. (The manager) drove members of my team and myself through many hours of extreme pressure to turn around project work on an unreasonable timeframe and without appropriate support from other organizations. Then without any explanation when the deliverable was done and completed decides not to use the work but to do something else. Not only was it demoralizing to the team but as the manager I found out from my team members who heard about it second hand.

In contrast, the worst manager is the direct opposite. He does not communicate at all with subordinates and other members of the team. Furthermore, when I try to communicate with him, he does not listen. I then try to document our conversations by e-mailing him conclusions of discussions (i.e. Once you review my work as discussed, I would like to meet with you at 3pm to discuss.). Yet, the manager does not keep to the plan nor does he communicate the fact that he cannot review/meet at the agreed upon times. I have found myself staying at work until all hours of the night because he says that he will address a project that I have done and most times, he just gets side-tracked and doesn't get to it. I have to remind him and check on his status constantly. I believe that I shouldn't have to do this. As a result, the inefficiencies are immense and unacceptable.

Examining the totality of communication-related responses revealed that the GEMs were excellent communicators. They were *good listeners* who were available and responsive to their co-workers and *gave clear and helpful feedback*, all within the bounds of a healthy and developmental relationship. The good enough manager *facilitated* by encouraging autonomy in employees while staying connected and engaged. Through these back and forth interactions a trusting relationship evolves that enables both the manager and employee to do their best work in their respective roles. By being emotionally attuned, the GEM elicits more details of a problem that can ultimately lead to more creative and effective approaches and eventual solutions. The following examples demonstrate how all of these qualities work together.

My best manager to date was a good listener, had reasonable expectations, provided guidance when needed, and had confidence in my abilities. Whenever she assigned me a project, she allowed me to execute it without interfering unnecessarily. If I needed assistance, she was always willing to listen and provide guidance. For example, I was in charge of developing content for a monthly newsletter. At the beginning of each month, she and I would sit and discuss what content should be included. She would make suggestions, but allowed me to make decisions, too. Once we decided on what should be included, I was allowed to run with the newsletter – writing articles, working with other contributors, and collaborating with the graphic designer. While she had the ultimate editorial authority for the newsletter, and sometimes made edits to the content, she was always reasonable about the changes and listened to me if I disagreed.

As director of sales, this manager always was clear and direct, ran efficient meetings and was willing to adapt to new ideas and opportunities. Importantly, while he may have collected information from other sources it always was clear that his opinions and his views were based on his personal observations, perceptions, experiences and analyses. A specific example of the manager's excellence is the approach that he took upon assuming leadership of a distributed team of sales professionals. He had a dozen managers each with a dozen staff members and he took the time to meet first with all of the managers and then with every member of every manager's team. He didn't have to do this. Some expressed the opinion that it was too much time with the troops and not enough productivity. But, the result was a very effective organization because the manager had become familiar with each of the players and them with him. That facilitated much more open communication among the entire group. The difference was in the rapport (trust) that this manager had created simply by listening intently, following through on commitments he made and letting folks know that he would trust them and they could trust him. That knowledge lit up the team. On a personal level, he created a close, professional relationship with me that was built upon his expressed understanding of my skills and the value that I represented to him and the organization as well as a set of mutual commitments that we made to one another to support team goals and to communicate effectively in all circumstances.[17]

The best manager is someone that gets to know the type of person you are on a professional level and on a somewhat personal level and can "read" you better than you think. I think of one person in particular that I consider to be my best manager – he was funny, considerate, knowledgeable, and a great listener. The one incident that comes to mind was during a personal time in my life where things seemed as though they were piling up in a negative way for me. I had come into work, as usual, and was trying to cope as best as I could. Without asking questions, my manager asked me to come into his office. He told me to take the rest of the week off to clear my head – he wasn't going to charge it as vacation time either – he just knew that I needed to get away. I came back after the weekend – the only question he asked was if I was ok and if I needed more time ... he never asked what had happened or what was wrong. He was patient and let me know that his door was always open.

An incident to illustrate a "best" manager: Recently I have been trying to resolve issues with a shared services department, that provides IT and Accounting services to our business unit, that has not been listening to the needs of business users and providing services that do not fit our requirements. For a few months as project manager (and acting business systems manager) I've been fighting the smaller battles myself, but it is becoming clear that there is a big picture issue with the current structure of project management and support provided by shared services. As this big picture became clear, I have approached my manager for assistance in clarifying the current issues and planning a path to resolution. In this process my manager has: 1) Taken a significant amount of time out of his schedule to listen to the issues. 2) Asked great questions to understand both sides of the issue. 3) Allowed me to make, own, and document suggestions for the resolution without stepping in and taking the issue to upper management. I will also be presenting the current issues and proposed resolutions to upper management. 4) Has pushed me to look at the situation from other directions to find other paths to resolution. Overall, my manager has taken the time to listen to and understand the issues, allowed me to continue my ownership of the project, and allowed me to build my skills as a project manager.

Micro-managing, on the other hand, was associated with poor listening, disrespectful behavior, and resistance to new ideas.

My manager never listened or showed attention. My boss would be on her blackberry while I was having a one-on-one review session or expressing concerns I have. It was tough. I also never had clear expectations on what I was working on. A lot of the time I spent hours working on something that was never even looked at.

He had no boundaries. He would call my cell at 11pm. He would not listen but instead had his own agenda. He often got caught up in details that were irrelevant and unimportant to the final task. I would be exhausted after just talking to him because I had to work so hard to try to get him to understand what I needed to be successful.

He told us how to do our jobs EXACTLY the way he would do it, rather than let us make our own managerial decisions. He was not open-minded to new ideas and everything I did that wasn't exactly how he would have done it was "wrong." He also didn't listen to our feedback and it was very frustrating when he would be typing up an email while we were talking to him about communicating better in the office.

Feedback

Those described as best managers provided feedback that was timely, specific, and helpful both to the task and the growth and development of the employee. It was seen as part of the mentor/teacher role and delivered in a way that was honest, direct, and respectful as these examples illustrate:

My best manager provided me with feedback that was timely and specific. For example, instead of saying "Great job!" my best manager says "Great job with your presentation. You were very articulate and detail focused, while engaging the audience." This also gives a manager an opportunity to provide constructive feedback in addition to the positive comment. He may add "Next time, it would be even better if you slowed things down a bit to let the audience digest it a bit more. Overall, nice work!" Also, providing specific instructions on a task is helpful. This alleviates unnecessary back and forth when a manager delegates. It is very useful when a manager provides the overall goal of a task or project, which enables me to make more educated decisions without getting my manager involved.

Gave me feedback and advice privately. Always supported me publicly (meetings, presentations, comments when I wasn't present, etc). Often told a story from his personal experience when giving direction and concluded with "If I were you, I would…" then gave his advice. I always felt that I made the final decision to follow his direction or not (of course I always did because it was always sound advice). I felt valued and respected, an important part of the team. Here's one specific story. I only had a year of experience and was brand new in this position. I sent out a report that later I found a mistake in and had to resend the email with the report. Afterwards he showed me some ways to proof reports, told me a story of a similar "error" that he had made early on and said that I should be absolutely certain things were correct before distributing them because I would gain an image of being a reliable and trusted source for info. It was good advice and delivered in a way I could listen to without getting my hackles up.

When respondents referred to their worst managers, feedback was also a significant part of their experience, although in these cases the feedback was either non-existent or handled poorly by focusing on trivial issues (such as paper clips), or delivering the information in a condescending way.

> I would explain this person as the worst manager because the individual does not provide me with the time of day to help advance both my understanding of the material I am working on, as well as not providing me with time to ask career based questions. The individual is extremely condescending and is very rude, if they notice a mistake. This individual does not communicate any negative feelings directly to me; instead the individual chooses to write it in my written feedback, or bring up my poor performance at an important meeting, without notifying me that I had made an error, or should have been working late/weekends. Overall, the individual lacks the ability to communicate effectively with me for both positive and negative issues.

> The worst manager is one who talks about providing support for you in your job, but does not become engaged with your work unless I bring it to her attention. Outside of issues which come up, she has no intent in understanding what your job responsibilities include. The communication is always up to her and rarely is she asking about how things are going. She doesn't communicate until required, not reaching out to find out how things are going on a regular basis, no scheduled meetings to determine where the entire group stands with tasks that require completion. Recent Example: I had a presentation to a senior executive regarding a new technology within our industry. I requested some time with her to give her a "dry run" with what was to be presented, and she wasn't concerned or engaged to submit any feedback on what was going to be presented. I personally was hoping she could provide some insight on what would work with this executive in terms of presentation since she has had significant dealings with him in the past. The "dry run" never happened and there was never a call after the presentation to me to see how things went.

> My worst manager was constantly looking for mistakes/failures. She would "plant" work to see if I would just pick it up and do it, and if I didn't, that was a failure on my part. Although at the time, I was an

adult with a college degree, I was treated as a child. I had to ask to go to the bathroom or take a lunch break. At the end of the day I was expected to ask if there was anything else that I could do for her before I left. If so, I was expected to stay, on her whim, sometimes several hours. Feedback was only given at annual assessment, and was most often negative (and no/very small raise). When I would ask why feedback was not given more frequently, so that I could improve over the course of the year, I was told that she didn't care enough to do so.

I had my "worst" manager early in my career. He was the type that sat in his office and did not make time to understand his staff. His focus was always on the project schedule. He did not mentor his staff. He always gave the impression his assignment was temporary as he moved up the corporate ladder. At weekly one-on-one meetings, he did not provide performance feedback. During a large project I was working on, I was responsible to test a system conversion program. It was the first time I had done this type of testing. My manager did not monitor my progress or review my test plan/results. Ultimately, we experienced major problems at conversion. Although I felt horrible on my own and spent many hours trying to correct the problems, my manager made me feel worse. Although the team recovered from the conversion problem, the blame was put on me. As a result, I experienced surprises at my year-end evaluation. While working for him, I had my worst evaluation in my 20 year career. It damaged my reputation with senior staff which took at least two years to prove myself again.

I had a manager who would not give me any feedback and had a lot of absences in which she had taken work I needed home. One good example was that I was marked down in a review for using paperclips on my reports ... every morning I would give her my reports paper-clipped so she could review and sign off where needed. After reviewing the reports she'd hand them back to me to file stapled and return the paper-clips to me. After six months of this I had my review and it was then she finally mentioned that she wanted the reports stapled and marked it against me in the review.

My worst boss had no leadership skills. He had been a good developer who was promoted to manager of two small development teams. I was lead developer for one of those teams. I was responsible for the roll-out of the first in-house developed application. This also included the design and creation of user documentation. So as not to design in a bubble, I elicited feedback from my boss. I provided my boss with copies of the proposed documentation as it was being created. This included page layouts, screenshots, and text to tell users how to use the system. At all times, I invited feedback from him. None was received, so we moved forward. The documentation was submitted for printing and binding; then distributed to the user community. The second in-house application was due to be released. Its documentation used that produced for the first application as its template. A copy of the documentation was provided to my boss for review. No response. The documentation was submitted for printing and binding. It was in my office for distribution to the user community. Work on the documentation for a third application was underway. My boss came to my office one day with the copy of the first application's documentation that I had given him. He had made notes with his required changes. The entire layout changed. We could use nothing of the template. I was told to gather all the previously released documentation and redo it as well as any subsequent documentation. I was in shock and very angry. He couldn't give his feedback months ago! Yes, I wasn't happy about the layout change, but my team had wasted so many man hours, never mind the waste of paper and humiliation of having to gather all the old documentation back before we could (create) new documentation. He was eventually moved to another position; those poor people.

Taken together, all of these examples demonstrate that the GEMs are powerful relationship builders who create and nourish working environments characterized by clear and consistent communication, active listening, and careful instructive feedback, all serving to affirm interactions based on trust and mutual respect. These findings reinforce current research on factors that lead to happiness in different areas of life. Dan Beuttner, a writer and National Geographic explorer, traveled the world and discovered "blue zones," those areas that have the longest life expectancy and general happiness. He notes that relationships play a key role in the happiest societies, with the happiest people in America socializing, that is, having meaningful interactions with others, around seven hours a day. The main determinant of enjoying one's work experience, even more than pay, is the presence of a best friend in the workplace, and Beuttner recommends that individuals take the initiative to build good work relationships by organizing happy hours or other social activities.[18] The GEMs know the value of work as a social process and build the kinds of relationships that enhance work as a central ingredient of a fulfilling life.

five

GEMs as Models of Integrity

Do the right thing. It will gratify some people and astonish the rest.

—Mark Twain

In their book entitled *Leaders*, Warren Bennis and Burt Nanus observed that the problem with many organizations is that they are over-managed and under-led, meaning that the emphasis is often more on handling the daily routines rather than questioning whether the routines are even appropriate or desirable. This dilemma moved them to present the following distinction: *managers are people who do things right and leaders are people who do the right thing.*[1] Managers, in their view, are more concerned about efficiency while leaders focus more on vision and judgment, or effectiveness. Although intended to distinguish between the mechanical technocrat shuffling papers and following procedures, and the thoughtful visionary at the helm, the juxtaposition of manager *versus* leader presents a false dichotomy because the "best" bosses or managers must be concerned with, and proficient in, both domains. As we saw in Chapter 1, managers can be leaders and vice versa. The trains have to run on time, to borrow a well-worn metaphor, but those who run the trains also have to know where they are going and why.

Because of their greater emotional investment and ability to relate to others, *good enough managers* naturally lean more in the direction of the "leader" in these terms. Viewing the process of managing as a "performing art," Peter Vaill sees the central concern of leadership *and* management as values clarification. Leadership is the articulation and energetic presentation of new values and is a teaching and coaching process. The more day-to-day process of management involves the discovery and working through of value conflicts. Managers seek harmony among existing elements while leaders seek to change the elements, and like Escher's drawing hands, each set of actions is indispensable to the other. In an article about teaching – one of the cornerstones of good enough managing – I once put it this way: "Good tools and technical proficiency are essential to performing any task well; however, the difference between performing a task and producing a work of art is the amount of the performer's soul that is transfused in the process."[2]

Doing the Right Thing

One can justifiably ask the whereabouts of the souls of many modern-day leader-managers. We have just begun to emerge from a period of organizational mismanagement and near financial collapse. Beginning with the downfall of Enron and WorldCom, and other corporate scandals in the early part of the decade, to the recession of 2007–8, we have seen all kinds of organizational malfeasance and excesses of great magnitude. From Bernie Madoff's elaborate and massive Ponzi scheme that lost billions of dollars for investors, to the financial machinations such as credit default swaps and sub-prime mortgages that contributed to the bursting of the housing bubble and subsequent financial decline, we have to question the role of managers in these events. Were they asleep at the wheel or just going along for the ride?

While these events are continuing to unfold, it is clear that the causes of the crisis are manifold and interconnected: too much debt, too little regulation, and a complicit and enabling culture. Malcolm Gladwell suggests that overconfidence was at the heart of the debacle, especially in the world of finance where such an overly optimistic attitude is often useful and adaptive.[3] But, it can also create an illusion of invulnerability that leads to excessive risk taking. As Gladwell concludes:

> Perhaps this is part of why we play games: there is something intoxicating about pure expertise, and the real mastery we can attain around a card table or behind the wheel of a racecar emboldens us when we move into the more complex realms. "I'm good at that. I must be good at this, too," we tell ourselves, forgetting that in wars or on Wall Street there is no such thing as absolute expertise, that every step taken toward mastery brings with it an increased risk of mastery's curse.[4]

Add to this a perceived "winner-take-all" society, a growing wealth gap between the very rich and the rest of society that can undermine our social fabric, and excessive pressure to succeed, and we enter the realm of what some social observers have labeled a "cheating culture." As the media, also under greater economic pressure, chase ratings and fixate on "infotainment" and the adventures and misadventures of the rich and famous (some famous for being famous), overconfidence often morphs into hubris. The larger culture attributes moral superiority to those who achieve material success, even by questionable means. The tendency to cheat or cut corners trickles down to ordinary middle class citizens who become insecure and cynical while trying to get ahead.[5] Such hubris practiced by managers is based on an illusion of certainty and invulnerability, key ingredients of "groupthink," the social phenomenon leading to a breakdown of critical thinking in group decision-making, resulting in ineffective or even disastrous decisions such as the Bay of Pigs invasion or the Challenger explosion.[6] With a worldview that essentially proclaims that vulnerability is for losers, doing the right thing and working with a sense of ethics, social responsibility and humility becomes increasingly rare.

Vulnerability does not have to be a toxic asset. A prime example of doing the right thing was provided years ago by William Peace in his managerial memoir published in the *Harvard Business Review*.[7] A former general manager of the Synthetic Fuels Division at Westinghouse in the 1980s, Peace, a self-described "soft" manager, tells the story of a difficult period when Westinghouse discontinued its synthetic fuels business, resulting in the laying off of several employees with the goal of best positioning the business for eventual sale. He details how the 15 employees were selected for the layoff, a painstaking process, and the plan of informing them of the bad news. Instead of leaving the task to subordinates or an impersonal letter from the Human Resources department, Peace decided to face the employees himself to explain the reasoning for the move and to answer their questions. He describes walking into a funereal conference room, fielding direct questions from employees, and responding to their inevitable anger and sadness. As he recalled,

> I felt a certain new closeness to those 15 people. I shook hands with each of them and wished them good luck. I thought I sensed that most of them understood and even respected what we were trying to do however much they might object to our final choice of sacrificial lambs.[8]

The story continues as the business was sold and the new owner gave funds for enough additional work so that the 15 laid off employees could be rehired. All of them accepted the offer to return, even some who had already taken on new jobs.

Although this experience took place in the 1980s, it has particular relevance as organizations are currently experiencing numerous layoffs as a response to the current economic crisis. Peace attributes the success of his approach in large part to the fact that by engaging the affected employees personally and directly, he made himself vulnerable to their strong emotions of anger and disappointment. Although he used the term "soft" manager, meaning one who is open and non-defensive in relation to the experience of his employees, he is describing the essence of a GEM. He lived his values of openness and candor and showed his respect for his employees. And, he took the heat without melting or exploding. As he concludes, "tough management does not necessarily mean effective management. Self confidence can be a cover for arrogance or fear, resolute can be a code word for autocratic, and hard-nosed can mean thick skinned."[9]

Values and Integrity

Consider the following story of "Cassie," described by an employee as one of the "worst" managers:[10]

> Cassie was entirely incompetent in her role as VP of Sales, a problem compounded by her not having the wits even to attempt to conceal that fact from her subordinates, peers, superiors, customers or prospects. She routinely would berate, belittle and demean members of her team. She once called a meeting of all team members, including those who lived across the country and required in-person attendance (on short notice, during the holidays). Then she decided that she would run the meeting from home, via speakerphone. The results were not good. The team did unite that day, but it was not the kind of union that advanced the business or that aided her personal or professional development. Cassie did not know the business, the market, or much about technology though she led a team of high performing sales pros, many with advanced degrees and all of whom took great pride in being well-informed in all aspects of the business. In short she commanded no respect, she offered no respect and she made no efforts to earn respect or trust. There were of course some classic, memorable moments. There was the time that she tried to motivate one of the top performers for many years before her arrival. She had just cut his territory and handed him a sharply reduced compensation plan. During the ensuing discussion, she saw the opportunity to light a fire under him with the query "Don't you think your wife would love you more if you made more money?" There was the day that she told another employee, the team's administrative assistant, to "go to (a variety store) and get this stuff" then handed her the school supplies list for her fourth grade son. Or the day she sent the same employee back to the store to "get me some tampons." Another day she asked the (same) administrative assistant to add the items on an (office supply store) receipt to an expense report. When she inquired about some of the items, which included various craft supplies, and how to

record their business purpose, Cassie's response was: "They are for my kids – just say that they are for a team meeting." Integrity was not a strong point either. Mass departures began – the top performer was the first. Eventually, after most of us had left, Cassie was dismissed.

We see several inter-related elements at work in this rather unfortunate tale: Cassie's inflated sense of entitlement, abuse of power, the denigration of employees, and using them to obtain items for her personal needs and then lie about them on expense reports. There are hints that the entitled behavior is connected to her feelings of inadequacy and vulnerability in the managerial role, and her attempts to overcompensate for these unacknowledged feelings. It is particularly interesting that Cassie literally hid at home, conducting business by speakerphone after insisting that all team members drop their plans and report for a meeting during a holiday.

Let's compare that episode to the following story from a respondent about an exceptional manager, whom we will call Tom:

> This was a person of tremendous personal integrity, honor, competency, and applied sense of what is both RIGHT and just. Truly remarkable. A world-wide Vice President of Global Information Systems (VPGIS), Tom was forced out of his function by a much younger, ruthlessly ambitious, talented financial deal-doer who had undermined the Chief Financial Officer for his job and embarked on a disastrous merger and acquisition course ... while making himself Senior Executive Vice President in the process. Tom stood up to him based upon what was *right*. The Senior Executive Vice President hired a consultant from one of the huge CPA consulting giants to do an operations audit on Global Systems. Not only was this a hatchet job, the consultant "graciously" agreed to become the *new* V.P. of Global Information Systems based upon his "brilliant findings" (the Senior Executive V.P.'s words). In turning the reins over to this interesting fellow, Tom, the *now-former* VPGIS, gave one of the most eloquent speeches to his organizational leaders I've ever heard in my life. No rancor. Good of the company. Time for change. Support the new team as you have supported me all these years. There was not a dry eye in the place! Even the Senior Executive Vice President was stunned by the graciousness. The new, quite young V.P. for Global Information Systems stood and preened. The contrast was stark and more than a little alarming. NOW THEN: just two days later the Board Chairman walked into Tom's office as he was packing up and anointed him Vice President & General Auditor of the Corporation. (His) assignment: rebuild from scratch the old corporate audit function and use his knowledge of where all the bones were buried to get the company out of the gray areas of consent decrees, ethics,

corporate social responsibility, scandals, etc. The Senior Executive Vice President almost had a stroke. (The story continues.)

Shortly before this "consultant" had been hired by the Senior Executive V.P., I had been "rescued" from a horrible working situation by the Systems V.P., and sent on a special assignment to Washington, D.C. on loan to the Assistant Secretary of Commerce for Finance & Administration (because the Assistant Secretary had specifically asked for me and it was a great excuse to get me out of the line of fire of my former boss who was furious that I'd gotten away from his division, and had retaliated by not releasing my pay authorizations for a raise for an extra six months – just because he could do that). Ten months into my year-long Washington assignment, Tom, now General Auditor, called to say that he needed me and would I come back early. Of course (I responded)! But there was an initial big price: the Senior Executive V.P. personally called me to say how disappointed he was in my decision to go to Audit rather than take a better-paying post in Information Management & Control under the new Global Information Systems V.P. My career was dead. But I'd given my word to Tom. In 14 months, this remarkable human being built what was then regarded nationally as one of the ten best corporate audit functions in the U.S. It was most curious that he always called himself "just an East Texas farm boy ... what do I know about management?" ... Coincidentally, the Senior Executive Vice President got fired, as did the consultant/new V.P. Global Information Systems, as did a number of "bandwagon" types. Yet as one of his five direct reports, we never saw Tom plot personal vengeance. But we sure did see the unrighteous fall! He never abused his authority, yet the clarity of his work and his pursuit of ethics was astonishing. (He was) one of the most human and compassionate professionals I've ever known.

Several themes intersect in these two complex situations. Although this story of Cassie showed up under the theme of "disrespect" covered in the previous chapter on relationships, it is also clear that the demeaning behavior was accentuated by a lack of integrity and ethics (noted in the opening sentence of the description) that ultimately contributed to her downfall as a manager. The second case, told from the perspective of a respondent caught up in an executive power play of Machiavellian proportions, depicts Tom, a senior manager who shows dignity, grace, humility, and a moral sense of "what is right" under the most difficult of circumstances. In this case the good guys may have initially lost the battle but they won the war, and the righteous prevailed.

Though not as dramatic as these, there were many other cases throughout the study where the demonstration of trust and mutual respect were also infused with a sense of managers living and acting upon some very basic values. These values are at our core, and are part of a human being's foundation formed in the earliest stages of life. They serve to form our moral sense, our assumptions or personal rules that guide our choices and behavior. We generally see morality as a developmental process of maturity. Kohlberg's well known progressive model of moral development begins with the pre-conventional level or the "self orientation" with two sequential stages: avoiding punishment for breaking rules (Stage 1), and seeking rewards for oneself (Stage 2). The person at this initial level begins to have awareness of others' needs, but not of right and wrong as abstract concepts. Moving to the next moral level, the conventional level, the individual focuses more on the other, and seeks to be a "good person" who is accepted by family and friends, but not to fulfill a moral ideal (Stage 3) and acting "right" to comply with law and order norms and societal institutions (Stage 4). The third level is the post-conventional, autonomous, and principles level or the "universal humankind orientation." The stages here emphasize the social contract: acting "right" by seeking consensus through due process and agreement and by appreciating the relativity of values and tolerating different points of view (Stage 5), and ultimately universal ethical principles: acting "right" according to universal abstract principles of justice and human rights (Stage 6). Here the person employs conscious moral reasoning to guide actions and decisions. Kohlberg's 20-year study revealed that most people reach the fourth and fifth stages by adulthood, but few attain the highest sixth stage.[11]

Psychologists researching value formation note remarkable similarities and consistencies across societies and cultures, and conclude that these values are deeply rooted in the unconscious mind. As David Brooks comments on this "intuitionist" view:

> Just as we have a natural suite of emotions to help us love and be loved, so, too, we have a natural suite of emotions to make us disapprove of people who violate social commitments and approve of people who reinforce them. There is no society on earth where people are praised for running away in battle.[12]

Cognitive psychologist Steven Pinker presents five core values that are embedded through evolution and constitute the "primary colors" of our moral sense:

1 *harm* – avoiding harming others and attempting to help them
2 *fairness* – reciprocating favors, rewarding benefactors, punishing cheaters
3 *community* – group loyalty, sharing and solidarity, conformity to norms
4 *authority* – deferring to legitimate authority, respecting those of higher status
5 *purity* – exalting cleanliness, loathing defilement, contamination and carnality.[13]

In similar fashion, Rushworth Kidder cites a similar set of value themes: *honesty, respect, responsibility, fairness,* and *compassion.*[14]

Although the word *ethics* pops up again and again in politics and in college business curricula, especially after a period of highly visible scandals such as Watergate or Enron, much of it is retrospective and reflexive, and seldom followed up with substantive action. Sometimes new laws and regulations are enacted, such as the Sarbanes-Oxley legislation, or there is a shift in political power that seeks to stabilize and correct the broken system. No doubt there will be a new emphasis and debate concerning regulatory structures in response to recent market excesses such as the recently enacted (but highly resisted) financial reform legislation in Congress. At the working level, however, ethics takes on a more personal tone. People respond to managers who live a principled life at work and put their values into daily practice.[15]

Since they are particularly attuned and responsive to others, the GEMs are naturally focused on the "mutuality" that is at the core of these relationships as explored previously. It would follow that they are more inclined to recognize and accept their own flaws and limitations, and take responsibility for their behavior in relation to others. Comments from the 1,058 respondents about the best and worst managers to the survey in Chapter 2 tapped into some of these value domains, as themes such as *fairness* (specifically mentioned in 77 cases) and *honesty* (68 cases) were prevalent in the best managers. Variations on these themes also showed up in the worst cases as *taking credit* for others' accomplishments (73 cases), *blaming* others (36 cases), and *playing favorites* (30 cases). Although it was implied in other forms, the actual word *dishonest* appeared alone in 18 cases.

Fairness

Fairness was a predominant theme often connected with other attributes such as trust, autonomy, and feedback. Here are a few representative descriptions and stories of managers who were considered fair in their dealings with co-workers:

> This manager displayed well both the "process" side as well as the "people" side of things. She was able to get a very good gauge of people and evaluate situations at a very high level. She was not a micromanager but allowed her reports the freedom to do their jobs, make mistakes, and learn from them. She was always available for assistance and readily gave feedback on performance so the report knew exactly where he/she stood. There was a time when the support staff was going through turmoil – they were understaffed when the office was projected to grow,

and many on the staff disliked the previous leadership and were very "gun-shy" after hearing about layoffs in the sister office. This manager came in and helped to build up the unity of the team – despite what the "numbers" said, she fought to get the team staffed with capable people and this base of solid employees are still thriving in the company today. Specific behaviors exhibited: open door policy, friendly, competent, fair, and transparent.

The best manager or boss I have worked for was very clear in her expectations of my work. She was fair and understanding as long as I communicated any problems or issues. She was quick to help out when there was too much work for one person to handle. When I had concerns about my work or my progression within my position, she would set aside time to meet and discuss ways that I could further my education at work, even when she was extremely busy. She allows me enough space to do what I need but is there when I have questions. And she always trusted me to do my job. She wasn't a micro-manager. One time, there was a project that I had to complete that came from the top of the organization. It was not all together pleasant because every time I thought I was done with it, someone would make the decision to change a format or some little thing that would take forever to change in all of the documents. The project became a mess. However, my boss managed it really well and asked where she could be the most help with formatting and finalizing the project. She didn't think that it was beneath her to help out even though the project was not very strategic or thoughtful.

As seen in this last description, the best managers demonstrated a sense of fairness by being willing to pitch in where needed, without concern about the work being beneath them in any way. There also seemed to be a genuine desire to help in a way that did not encroach on others, yet it served them well by building trust and respect and reinforcing the caring teacher role.

This person was the best manager because not only was she fair in almost all of her decisions, work assignments, and in dealings with department matters, but she rolled up her shirt-sleeves and pitched right in, doing work. She was in early, usually left about 5, but you knew she also worked a lot at home evenings and oftentimes weekends as well. She cared about you as an individual and also as a part of a team. She showed no favoritism amongst a department made up of mostly females. She retired, and it was not until after a few had attempted to take her position, did I truly realize how lucky I was to have worked with such a fine department manager as she. She had a lot of experience, was well educated, kept up on changes in tax law, and was always willing to listen and/or to help in any way that she could.

Fairness was also a common theme as it related to giving feedback and recognition. These managers were not interested in taking credit for others' successes and used feedback in a constructive and developmental way.

> This manager was "fair." When giving feedback, I always knew where I stood as far as my review. The feedback was specific, appropriate and measureable (SAM). When given my review I had both positive feedback but also areas to work on and nothing was a surprise to me. Also, this manager gave me credit where it was due and did not accept the credit on my behalf for what I had done. The quote "you are only as good as your people" is what she believed.

The theme of fairness showed up in the worst managers in the form of *taking credit* for others' accomplishments (alluded to in the above example), *blaming others* for mistakes, and *playing favorites*. Several of these ideas come together in the following rather cynical depiction of a worst manager situation:

> Although there wasn't a single worst manager for me, there were various other managers who had very severe bad management traits, those with the worst managerial practices, if we can call it that. In fact, I would go as far as to say that managers are usually bad managers. That's the norm. It's a matter of who is less bad than the other. Managers are usually accidental recipients of an award based on their loyalty for someone else, up above, and they then gain an undeserved stewardship over other people's work lives. They share "worst manager" traits. For instance, "worst managers" are usually not trained to be managers. So, they don't know how to assess subordinates' strengths and how to help them work through their weaknesses. They don't mentor, nor is it their role to develop others. Worst managers clearly pick favorites in the group and are not sensitive to his/her workers' own interests and ambitions. The very worst managers were clearly threatened by intelligent subordinates, had fear of other managers, thus were not great advocates for our team, played workers against one another, at times were deceiving and even retaliated against some workers who spoke out or criticized their decisions. Worst managers are usually not trained and are usually not held accountable by their organizations to develop their own workers. They were usually quite intelligent, but used it to play tricks on the less favorite, to find fault, to provoke. So, they were somewhat Machiavellian against those they disliked. So, they think mostly about themselves and their own

connections, which they believe will ensure their survival. Worst managers are precise clones or outcrops of the corporate cultures in which they flourish. Show me a "worst manager" and I will show you a company with no tradition for "breeding" good managers. Show me a company with a tradition for breeding good managers and you will have found a true exception.

According to this account, bad managers beget bad managers and the behavior becomes entrenched in a culture of suspicion, hostility, and scapegoating. The following stories about a pair of managers affectionately known as "cement head" and "the Teflon Lady" highlight how blame is often assigned. In one case the employee is blamed for the performance his boss thinks he should be doing but doesn't know; in the other, the blame is employed to deflect the boss's own shortcomings.

> I've actually had two "worst" managers, one male and one female. In each case, the person was my boss for less than a year – and in both cases I moved on (all within the same large company) to other opportunities. One quick story about each follows. The male (who his direct reports wound up calling "cement head" because he was so unimaginative and inflexible) gave me a performance review in which he started with my job description (JD) and noted that I did those things very well. He then pulled out a second sheet of paper and said it contained the tasks that he thought should be in my JD, and that I didn't do those things particularly well. He proceeded to formally evaluate me versus tasks (objectives) that I had not seen or been aware of prior to that day. He bristled when I asked him if he thought he was giving me a fair shake. The female (whom her direct reports came to call the "Teflon Lady" because nothing ever stuck to her) once reprimanded me in a staff meeting with our entire department (about ten people) watching. She was quite agitated to begin with, and then she started yelling at me when I asked her what she was talking about. It turns out that she was upset because an incorrect calculation had gone to her boss, and she blamed me for the error. She wasn't happy when I reminded her that I hadn't even touched that part of the information package in question – which she had handled herself. In a nutshell, she sought to embarrass me in front of my peers and then she lost it when I reminded her that she was the one who made the calculation error. This second episode strongly reinforced something I've always tried to practice: congratulate in public, reprimand in private.

Taking credit and assigning blame often appeared together, each reinforcing the other and revealing the underlying insecurity, avoidance of responsibility and deceitful practices of the manager, such as holding someone accountable for aspects of a job that were never communicated until the performance review. Here are two other examples that further illustrate the point:

> My worst manager was very power hungry and often stabbed others in the back to make herself look good. She never gave praise for anything good that was done, and often took the credit for work that other people did. There was one incident where she gave me direction to post a specific journal entry that I was not comfortable doing, because it went against all accounting rules that I have known. She insisted that was the correct thing to do, and as she was the CEO and a CPA, I did the entry. When the time came for the yearly audit, and they asked about the entry, she took NO credit for doing that entry, and led the audit partner and the board of directors to believe that I was the one that was responsible for doing the entry. As a result, the board of directors started to lose confidence in my decision-making and accounting skills, when the person who made the decision was HER. She never accepted responsibility for any decisions that she made that the board didn't like. Rather, she blamed other department heads.

> She was always in it only for herself. She would blame her shortcomings and mistakes on her staff members behind their backs and take credit for their successful ideas and accomplishments behind their backs. She was masterful at these tactics, but not masterful at her profession. She was sneaky and deceitful and obviously had no concern for anyone's success or well-being but her own. She was also not competent in the basics or organization and time management, often making her own lack of planning become everyone else's emergency. For example, on one occasion, she failed to inform several staff members about a department meeting in which each person would give a presentation on Monday morning. On Friday afternoon at a few minutes before the end of the day, she snuck pre-dated memos about the meeting into the in-boxes of the people she had not notified. Then she approached each person to "remind" them of the meeting and asked if their presentations were ready. We all knew what she had done, but we all had to cancel our weekends to come in to the office to prepare for the Monday meeting. She was so untrustworthy that no one who worked in her department respected her.

These managers have difficulty being genuine or authentic in their role. In an effort to fend off their feelings of inadequacy, insecurity and the anxiety of performing as a manager, they often resort to two very fundamental and interconnected human defenses:

1   *Splitting* the world into good and bad elements, resulting in playing favorites, creating a crony system, and denigrating others as threats. Children faced with the conflict of a loving parent who provides food and attention but also imposes limits or is sometimes absent, split the object that is the mother or father into the good parent and the bad parent. As one grows, one learns the important lesson that good and bad behavior (or behavior that we like and don't like) can simultaneously reside in one person. When confronted with stressful and anxiety provoking experiences, these more primitive defenses are evoked, resulting in a manager creating the idealized favorite employee and the others who just can't seem to do anything right. Popular culture in the forms of literature and movies and even politics (remember Richard Nixon's enemies list?) and sports are cast as a struggle between good and evil, heroes and villains, conservatives and liberals, and long-standing rivalries such as the Boston Red Sox and the New York Yankees.

2   *Projecting* one's own negative feelings such as insecurity and anxiety onto others, leading to a culture of blame and persecution. It is a way of getting rid of or avoiding unbearable thoughts and feelings, such as failure and rejection. If we have split the world into good and bad, it is easier to assign or attribute one's own weaknesses onto a perceived threatening presence, such as a younger manager seemingly after an elder's job or the lazy and incompetent employees who can't seem to get their act together and support the manager's goals.[16]

Many of the so-called "worst managers" were described in terms of what is commonly known as narcissistic behavior. Derived from the Greek myth of Narcissus, a beautiful young man who became enamored with his own reflection in a fountain, psychologists and other social scientists apply the term to the regulation of self-esteem in interpersonal relations and note that there are both healthy and destructive elements.[17] Healthy narcissism, based on relatively secure self-esteem, can provide self-confidence and the resilience to survive the frustrations and stress of daily managerial life, including failure to achieve goals and criticism from others. It also provides the fuel for empathy, the ability to form intimate and sustaining relationships, and the capacity to inspire others. On the destructive side of narcissism, outward displays of self-confidence can stem from grandiosity as a way to cope with fragile self-esteem and inner emptiness. There is an inflated sense of importance and entitlement, resulting in the devaluing and exploitation of others.

The inability of destructively narcissistic managers to form true and meaningful relationships combined with a lack of a personal set of values, along with inner emptiness, can lead to excessive risk taking and the manipulation of others to get ahead. These managers simultaneously seek admiration and idealize those above them as a way to merge with and identify with their power and prestige. The destructively narcissistic manager can also be highly suspicious and distrustful of others, and hypersensitive and argumentative as they tend to project their own weaknesses onto others who they suspect have hidden and threatening motives. They tend to surround themselves with enabling lieutenants who provide loyalty and praise and reinforce the impression of strength and competence. Because they are good at working the system, these managers can be highly adaptive and successful in certain organizations and can rise quickly in these systems, much to the detriment and dismay of those who have to work with and for them.

Eventually, their ploys, bullying, and scapegoating of others, credit-stealing and excessive impression management, and administrative practices that vacillate between the extremes of over-delegating and micro-managing catch up and take their toll, but not without causing a lot of pain, destroyed relationships, as well as lower productivity and poor succession planning.[18] It is very difficult to deal with destructively narcissistic managers because they do not respond to honest efforts to provide feedback and will often retaliate if their fragile self-esteem is threatened, especially by those beneath them in the organization. The employees must take a defensive posture, making sure to carefully document their actions and performance in case the manager attempts to undermine them for their own gain. It can be exhausting and diverts energy from the creative pursuit of the task. The only other alternative is to remove oneself from an intolerable situation, as many of the respondents did, by seeking a transfer or by quitting. In an economy where new opportunities are scarce, many people decide to make do with a bad situation, keep their heads down, and avoid making waves. The downside of such a false self strategy is resentment and cynicism that can only intensify the game-playing, and perpetuating a toxic culture.

The Authentic Manager

The GEMs create a "culture of authorization" in which the managers exercise not only their organizational authority, but also their *personal authority* in relation to their employees and co-workers. As Lawrence Gould states:

> Personal authority is experienced when individuals feel entitled to express their interests and passions, when they feel that their vitality and creativity belong in the world, and when they readily accept the power and vitality of others as contributions to their own experience. They give themselves and others permission to be vital, or in a word, to be authentic-in-role.[19]

GEMs are not threatened by others' ideas and passions but see their expression as part of a mutual relationship. They are able to experience and understand their own limitations and fallibilities and do not look to others as scapegoats or repositories to take the blame for their or the team's short-comings. They are also comfortable sharing the spotlight and giving credit where it is due. They have a sense of fairness and justice deeply rooted in their core values. It boils down to taking responsibility across several dimensions.

Behavioral responsibility – GEMs take responsibility for their own behavior and look to themselves first to see how they might be affecting a situation before targeting others as the source of the problem.

Emotional responsibility – GEMs have a tolerance for and the capacity to contain powerful emotions that arise as part of working in modern complex organizations, including uncertainty, and the anxiety that comes with con-stant change and environmental turbulence. By being able to accept these emotions in themselves and others, the GEMs create the zone of safety or the holding environment that is the hallmark of good enough managing. Employees feel freer to speak truth to power without fear of retribution, knowing that the GEM will not melt, self-destruct, or lash out and retaliate in some form.

Ethical and moral responsibility – GEMs serve as the moral center of their organization. This goes beyond minimal compliance and following the rules (important as they are), but negotiating and at times re-negotiating the boundaries of acceptable behavior. They set the moral tone and serve as an inspiration to others.

Interdependent responsibility – GEMs know that they are connected to a larger community and no matter how brilliant or accomplished, they cannot go it alone. They take an institutional view, looking at connections and rela-tionships with stakeholders across established boundaries, both inside and outside the organization.

Beyond exercising multiple levels of responsibility, the GEMs in this study served as paragons of *integrity*, a concept not widely mentioned in the management literature. One definition seems very consistent with many of the themes identified in the study:

> communicating clearly and consistently, being an honest broker, keeping promises, knowing oneself and avoiding hidden agendas that hang others out to dry. It comes very close to what we used to call honor, which in part means not telling lies to yourself.[20]

GEMs are inherently wise people, understanding and appreciating human frailties, most especially their own, and approaching others with a sense of acceptance, humility, dignity, and grace.

six

Becoming a GEM

Be patient toward all that is unsolved in your heart and try to love the *questions themselves* like locked rooms and like books that are written in a very foreign tongue. Do not now seek the answers, which cannot be given you because you would not be able to live them. And the point is, to live everything. *Live the questions now.*

–Rainer Maria Rilke

The previous chapters have identified through careful study the components of what it takes to be a good enough manager. The stories and narratives illustrate a fairly consistent repertoire of behaviors that focus on the role of managers as teachers and mentors who develop and maintain an open, supportive, yet accountable, relationship with their employees. These managers promote autonomy within well-defined and effectively communicated performance expectations and provide clear and helpful feedback on performance. They are aware of what is happening within themselves and their employees and do not try to control or micro-manage every aspect of a situation, but are ready to step in when necessary. They engender trust and respect through their actions and interactions. They are emotionally authentic, tolerant of uncertainty, adaptive to change, and accepting of their own limitations and imperfections in the face of an ever-changing and turbulent environment. They encourage creative thinking and learning from inevitable mistakes. They are perceived as fair and honest in their dealings with others and remain a touchstone for their employees, long after the formal reporting relationship ends.

It is logical to ask, are these GEMs just special people who walk among us or can one aspire to and even become one of these valuable managers?

After over 30 years of teaching interpersonal concepts and skills, I believe that it is indeed possible to become a GEM. I also believe the kind of learning required goes well beyond a training program or academic curriculum. Rather, it is an ongoing quest that requires personal reflection, constant practice and productive engagement with others. This chapter highlights the essential facets to be explored, drawing upon what we have learned about GEMs so far, and speaks directly to practicing and aspiring managers.

The journalist Bill Moyers stated that creative managing requires four major components:

1 Showing up
  Although Woody Allen is often credited with the idea that 80% of life is simply showing up, in this sense it means being an active and engaged presence.
2 Listening carefully
  The most effective managers are active, curious and empathic listeners.
3 Speaking the truth
  Communicating clearly and saying what needs to be said is an important skill, even if the message is not what everyone wants to hear.
4 Letting go of pre-determined results
  Moving beyond the status quo and venturing into unknown territory requires the ability to let go.[1]

These elements have a familiar ring of the GEMs described and discussed in the previous chapters as they focus on thoughtful presence, skilled engagement, and good communication. The identification and understanding of GEMs can be further translated into guidelines and lessons devised to enable anyone in the role of manager to develop and improve their performance. Building and expanding on Moyers's ideas, I have organized the ideas and lessons in this chapter around four key themes:

1 *Capacity* – building a reflective way of thinking based on the knowledge of one's own emotional intelligence, and orientation and understanding of oneself in a managerial role in relation to others.
2 *Competence* – understanding particular interpersonal skills that enable one to listen to others, communicate ideas and emotions, and then applying these skills in combination to engage others in solving problems, managing conflict and accomplishing the task in relation to organizational goals.
3 *Character* – appreciating one's own core values and mobilizing one's moral self in the managerial role.
4 *Commitment* – putting passion and purpose to work every day, connecting one's work with the larger community in a spirit of continuous learning.

Each of these "Four Cs" will be explored, building on the knowledge gained from the findings of the study, along with my reflections about the interpersonal nature of management gleaned from over 30 years of teaching and research.

Capacity

The capacity to be a GEM requires the manager to draw on his or her own inner resources, the human and personal qualities that are applied in the managerial role in relation to others. As we have seen in the employee responses, a greater proportion of these qualities comprise emotional resources as GEMs display empathy toward others, and are very open and tolerant of ambiguity and uncertainty in relation to the task as well as the larger organization and external community. As teachers and mentors, they create a learning environment in which each participant develops and applies his unique skills, and grows as an employee and human being.

Discovering Your Inner Teacher

It was clear from the perspective of those who participated in the study that the role of mentor is a central element of being a GEM. It can be seen as an act of *generativity*, of giving oneself to the development of the next generation of leaders, and creatively and productively moving the organization forward.[2] One of the most crucial tasks of being a manager, along with being a strategist and executor, is human capital development, managing talent and building long-term competencies in employees.[3] Mentoring has been shown to be a primary way to create and sustain a learning organization.[4] In addition to enhancing the career development of employees, it is also a vehicle to promote collaboration and openness in organizational relationships. As seen in the previous chapters, much of the behavior that characterizes GEMs (such as developing relationships, trust, and clear communication), occurs within a mentoring relationship.

Leadership is infectious and virally permeates throughout the levels of an organization.[5] GEMs beget other GEMs; many of the stories depicted ongoing relationships and a desire of employees to emulate what they have experienced from their bosses and pass it along. One of the main reasons that William Peace, the Westinghouse manager depicted in the previous chapter, was able to openly deal with his employees under tough circumstances was the influence of his mentor, Gene Cattabiani. As a general manager in the Westinghouse Steam Turbine Division in the 1970s, Cattabiani humanized a very contentious labor-management culture by exposing himself to open hostility and gradually winning over his adversaries. He created open dialogue where there was chronic animosity by being a human and credible presence, and eventually he was able to introduce more work flexibility along with higher standards that led to improved performance.[6] In this kind of relationship, the mentor serves not just as role model, but also as a teacher. As Daniel Goleman observed:

> Leaders have always played a primordial emotional role. No doubt humankind's original leaders – whether tribal chieftains or shamanesses – earned their place in large part because their leadership was emotionally compelling. Throughout history and in cultures everywhere, the leader in any human group has been the one to whom others look for assurance and clarity when facing uncertainty or threat, or when there's a job to be done.[7]

While most managers do not necessarily think of themselves as teachers, it is important for them to realize how crucial this role is in creating and sustaining a productive culture that often regenerates itself. In the give-and-take of a mentor relationship, a manager can reveal strengths and opportunities in employees that lay dormant but can come to life under the right circumstances. The idea of the "un-thought known" means that we all have capacities and emotional experiences that are waiting to be discovered and revealed, and they are often evinced through our interactions with significant others in particular settings. It is related to Winnicott's notion of the awakening of the true self – the genuine self – that harkens back to our earliest life experiences.[8] Managers can learn ways to do this by observing actual teachers, considering the essence of what it takes to be an excellent teacher, and building many of those qualities into their managerial role. They can discover their "inner teacher."

The *capacity* of a teacher is based on the complex interaction of the teacher's knowledge of the subject matter, the learning environment he creates for his students, and the students' abilities and responses in the working relationship. As Robert French and Peter Simpson explained, *Learning takes place at the edge between knowing and not knowing*.[9] The teacher and, by extension, the good enough manager, is poised on this boundary. The willingness to let go of the immediate desire for quick answers and to keep an open mind is central to this view of providing an effective learning environment, whether in the classroom or conference room. As will soon be seen, the human qualities of curiosity and empathy provide the foundation for significant learning interactions.

Consider these two reflections on the process of teaching by recognized master teachers:

> (The most effective teachers) ... became frustrated with students at times, and occasionally displayed impatience, but because they were

willing to face the failures of teaching and believed in their capacity to solve problems, they tried not to become defensive with their students or build a wall around themselves. Instead they tried to take their students seriously as human beings and treated them the way they might treat any colleague, with fairness, compassion, and concern. That approach found reflection in what they taught, how they taught it, and how they evaluated students, but it also appeared in attempts to understand their students' lives, cultures, and aspirations.[10]

In my efforts to understand, to really understand where my students are, I find it necessary to move beyond the demographic composition of the class or the student culture that exists at this point in time. I need to try to imagine what it is like being in their skin.[11] ... I aim at art, I'll settle for craft, but I'll not have a thing to do with science when it comes to teaching. That process in the classroom requires me to bring to it a kind of tactile familiarity all mixed up together so that in the moment I can synthesize it, largely unconsciously, and respond partly in awareness on the basis of intuitive skill in the moment as I see it.[12]

Substitute the word *manager* for *teacher*, *employee* for *student*, and *organization* for *class* in these quotes and we begin to see how GEMs exercise their teaching capacity.

Reflection-in-Action

GEMs have the ability to reflect, that is, to think about what they are doing while they are doing it. They are *participant-observers*, able to simultaneously be in the moment and also to step out of themselves and interpret or make sense of their experience, and then connect it to the interpretations of others in a larger context.[13] It is here that my thoughts turn to music as a metaphor for this kind of reflective capacity. Music is a transformation of emotional life and an avenue for understanding emotional expression in the art of managing and leading. Ron Heifetz and Marty Linsky provide this connection as follows: "Music is about moving people, about striking chords that resonate deeply in the hearts of listeners. It provides a language for elusive but central qualities like harmony, resolution, timing, improvisation, creativity, and inspiration."[14] As a lover of music residing in Boston, I have had the privilege of observing and appreciating some of the greatest symphony conductors in the world. The multiple talents and roles of these performers have often served as a metaphor for the practice of management. These musicians have a profound technical ability as they literally "know the score," but ultimately they are interpreters who extract and coordinate the musical elements and transform that meaning back to the orchestra and audience.

"Conductor" is a very appropriate word for this musical role because the music travels through them, they experience the music in the "here and now," and through this alchemy of verbal and nonverbal communication, translate a larger meaning to the audience. The result is often transformative and transcends individual performance.

Leonard Bernstein was a brilliant student, composer, and performer of music, a conductor who inhabited the music and, by his own observation, "became" the composer. Yet, as he often expressed, he was first and foremost a teacher who educated both the members of the orchestra, the audience, and the larger public through performances in numerous international concert venues, in the ground-breaking televised Young People's Concerts, and as a guest lecturer in residence at Harvard. He often described his "quasi-rabbinical" teaching instinct inherited from his father and influential teachers.[15] I recall watching him work with conducting students at the Tanglewood Music Center, a moment that revealed his essence as a teacher. He sat back and carefully observed as each student performed, and then through a very intimate one-on-one process, stretched their abilities, built their confidence, calmed their fears, and celebrated their successes. Many of these students and other protégés, such as Michael Tilson Thomas, John Mauceri, and Marin Alsop went on to have their own brilliant conducting careers and, in their own ways, carried on this teaching and mentoring role.

When James Levine became the music director of the Boston Symphony Orchestra, he also took on a natural teaching role. He worked the musicians hard in rehearsals, almost to the point of exhaustion and injury, stretching their abilities with his own prodigious musical knowledge. Through interactions with, and feedback from, the musicians he realized that he needed to take a step back, temper his approach, and adapt to their needs and limits. He also adapted his conducting style. In early performances he was more minimalist in his conducting movements, preferring that the audience focus their attention on the musicians and the music itself rather than on him as the performer. Over time he would become more active, depending on the needs of the musicians and the demands of the particular piece being performed. By the accounts of many long-term subscribers and reviewers, the BSO played at its highest level of performance through the bond with its musical leader.[16]

This willingness to adapt one's style to the moment was reinforced by a much younger conductor, Ludovic Morlot, a former assistant conductor for the BSO and currently music director of the Seattle Symphony. As one who has often served as a guest conductor for many orchestras, he has had to adapt very quickly, making the best of limited rehearsal time and working with musicians with whom he does not share history or deep knowledge. When asked about this challenge, he stated that with musicians of high expertise and experience, such as those in major symphony orchestras, he does not try to impose a rigid direction. Rather, he shares his overall ideas about the particular piece to be played at the beginning of rehearsal and lets the musicians play. As they play, he communicates more with his eyes and breathing than with his hands, more through feeling rather than by physically commanding his musical ideas.[17] The new music director of the New York Philharmonic, Alan Gilbert, has a similar philosophy, and ensures that the musicians buy into his vision. He asks for their ideas in relation to the result he is seeking by working through the senior musicians, capitalizing on the expertise and experience of the players, and keeping the music, the institution, and the audience as top priorities rather than his own personal gratification. Of course, this approach may be especially facilitated by the fact that one of those experienced musicians is violinist Yoko Takebe, Gilbert's mother.[18]

As with these musical leaders, a manager as interpreter brings to life two related processes that serve to create meaning and shared purpose: *sense-making*, the coalescing of information, insight and ideas into something meaningful, and *sense-giving*, a form of persuasion that communicates this meaning throughout the organization. The translation of ideas and belief systems up and down the organization is essentially a teaching function, using verbal language, nonverbal gestures, and symbols to shape the thinking and attitudes of others.[19]

This reflective or interpretive stance of a manager draws on two fundamental aspects of emotional intelligence: *emotional self-awareness* and *impulse control*. From Winnicott's perspective, the symphony conductor and the practicing manager create the holding environment as the containing vessel for the hard work of the task, and the productive release of strong emotions that animate the experience and translate it to others. Musicians, students, and employees need the manager to create this space in the tangible form of a downbeat, a syllabus, or a staff meeting agenda to guide and facilitate the exercise of talent and energy and then link it to the larger context of the organization and relevant environment. The manager is aware of his own emotional reactions and can manage or regulate these in the moment.

The key is to learn to understand emotions as a natural part of working. I often describe emotions to my students as a current that is always flowing within us. At times we can dip into this current, step back and try to understand what we are feeling and why. The stepping back to reflect can be envisioned as hitting the pause button long enough to feel what is happening before acting. First, we have to understand something about emotions. Scholars of emotional intelligence remind us that emotions are data, a signaling device that is part of our body's ancient way of alerting us to a threat or opportunity. Emotions are whole body experiences. We experience the body sensations such as the "heat" of anger, the rapid heartbeat of anxiety, the "pumped up" feeling of excitement, or the warm feeling of contentment and inner peace.

Getting to know one's body reactions is an important first step in gauging emotional reactions. This can be accomplished by the simple exercise of making a list of emotions such as anger, happiness, fear, anxiety, and sadness and then tracking the situation that elicited the feeling, the body sensations, and the associated thoughts that accompanied it. By understanding how these emotions are experienced, we can build a better foundation of awareness of what "pushes our buttons" or our "ouch points" that keep us from fully and productively engaging with others.[20]

Once we learn more about the experiencing of emotions, we can then enhance our capacity to manage them. Managing emotions does not mean becoming adept at ignoring or hiding them because the emotions will be working at a level beyond our awareness. We will be acting on these emotions less effectively and our body language will likely betray our valiant efforts to disguise them. One of the key aspects of emotional management is the ability to control impulses. This is particularly challenging when we feel stressed, as research shows that under duress we are more likely to act impulsively or seek immediate gratification, which may briefly work, but ultimately the negative feeling will likely return and the behavior or decision will likely cause additional problems.

Once again, it is time to hit the pause button, or in the world of instant and ubiquitous communication, to pause before hitting the "send" button. How many times have any of us immediately fired off a sharply worded rejoinder to an email, perhaps even copied a few choice people or even an entire distribution list, only to regret the electronic outburst later? Such impulsive behavior is not only alienating to co-workers, but frequently leads to apologies and efforts to mend the damage that often cannot be undone. Despite one's best efforts to implore people to disregard the email, such messages cannot be "unread." Many of the "worst manager" stories focused on managers who were quick to point fingers and assign blame or were hostile or condescending to their employees, usually in response to a situation that made them uncomfortable.

A casual viewing of the daily news can remind us that impulse control is often in short supply. Road rage and its variants (air rage, violent flash mobs) seem to be flourishing as modern life has gotten more complicated and frustration can easily mount. The demands for instant responses (why haven't you answered my email that I sent ten minutes ago?) compounded by the notions of "instant" messaging, snap polls concerning issues about which respondents have little or only superficial knowledge, and marketing targeted for impulse shopping, only make matters worse. Attention spans have dwindled and there is a desire to act and move on which continues to erode the value of reflection. Given these circumstances, admonitions like "look before you leap" seem quaint and prosaic, lest we fall behind in our race to somewhere. Yet, that is exactly what we must do, even if it goes against the tide. Patience is a rare commodity, so the GEMs that have the capacity to "hang" even for a moment are providing a valuable service.

It is here that a couple of thoughts are useful to keep in mind. One is *"ready, fire, aim,"* Harry Levinson's critique of management by impulse that reinforces the idea of reflecting and seeking ideas from others before taking immediate action.[21] The other is more personal. When I was receiving training as a psychotherapist, one of the most celebrated teachers of therapists in the Boston area, the late Anne Alonso, shared a significant piece of wisdom with her students: *don't just do something, sit there.* One of the most useful "instruments" of any therapist, and by extension, any teacher or manager, is to avoid the impulse to jump in and immediately start doing what others should be doing. I have observed neophyte teachers who try to create a Socratic discussion by posing a question and immediately answering it for their students. Better to get on to the next topic or slide so as to make sure all is "covered." Efficient, yes, but the students don't own or internalize their learning. The teacher wonders why so few students are participating in class or asking questions. The conductor does not play the music ... like the unthought known, he elicits and interpets it. Poor impulse control is the stuff of micro-managers. The GEMs intuitively know how to create a space and step back just enough to follow the ebbing and flowing rhythms as the work is performed. In this way, perhaps *reflection-in-action* is better expressed as *reflective inaction.*[22]

Empathy

As GEMs need to be in tune with their own emotional currents, they also must have the capacity to tune in to the world of others such as their co-workers, employees, managers, and clients or customers. Empathy is the word that usually captures this willingness and ability to go into the ideas and feelings of another person. But, it is an often misunderstood and, at times, misguided process. During the confirmation hearings for Supreme Court Justice Sonia Sotomayor in 2009, "empathy" became a code word for bias, as (for mainly political reasons) her detractors tried to show that she would show favoritism to particular groups of people, especially those sharing her Hispanic/Latina background. In nominating her, President Obama had indicated that he desired someone with empathy in addition to a keen legal intellect, meaning someone who would bring a variety of experiences to appreciate a range of ideas coming before the bench. As Sotomayor herself explained as she accepted the nomination:

> This wealth of experiences, personal and professional, has helped me appreciate the variety of perspectives that present themselves in every case that I hear ... It has helped me to understand, respect and respond

to the concerns and arguments of all litigants who appear before me, as well as to the views of my colleagues on the bench. I strive never to forget the real world consequences of my decisions on individuals, businesses and government.[23]

Despite her attempts to explain her judicial approach and philosophy, empathy had already been promulgated as a talking point to those wishing to cast her as racially biased and thus unfit to serve on the high court. Although Sotomayor was eventually confirmed, empathy as a professional human quality took a hit.

It is important to restore empathy as a cornerstone of emotional intelligence, human relations, and reasoned judgment. Ironically, it was another Supreme Court Justice, newly retired John Paul Stevens, who many years ago put forth a central process that he learned from his mentor, Justice Wiley Rutledge, and that is the habit of *understanding before disagreeing*.[24] Empathy is one's willingness and ability to see the world from the perspective of another person, even if that view is different from one's own perceptions and ideas, the proverbial "walking a mile in someone else's shoes." It is more than just being nice or sympathetic to another's situation or plight, desirable as those qualities are.[25] Empathy requires a suspension of one's own frame of reference, or the capacity to resist knowing or judging too quickly. Drawing upon John Keats's idea of "negative capability," Freud's notion of "evenly hovering attention," and the original German word *Einfuhlung* (or literally, "feeling into something," later imperfectly translated as *empathy*), Alfred Margulies provides this elegant definition: "The empathic exploration demands of the investigator the creative capacity to suspend closure, to know and not know simultaneously."[26] Once again the manager is on that boundary between knowing and not knowing. For a GEM, the emotionally intelligent quality of empathy requires both an active and passive way of relating to others: a *resonant* experience of the other (the emotional experience of being in another's presence) and the *imaginative* experience of searching for meaning in the feelings and ideas of an employee or co-worker. Put in more practical terms, an empathic manager can sense or experience the tension in the room at a meeting about a new policy, particularly with the one or two employees most directly affected. Rather than become defensive and write off the reactions to recalcitrance or even worse, remaining oblivious to their obvious discomfort, an empathic manager would try to imagine what this policy might mean in the world of these employees that is clearly different from his own. The latter process can enable the manager to put his inherent curiosity into action in the form of listening, a specific set of competencies of GEMs that we will explore later in this chapter. This enhanced understanding might lead to the kinds of conversations that can clarify the policy or enable the manager to build a better case to persuade reluctant or fearful employees. Empathy is the fuel of relationships and effective collaboration. It also contributes to the building of trust and respect, two qualities that were shown in the study to be essential to GEMs. It is also the basis for working with an increasingly diverse workforce and global environment and reducing prejudice, aggression, and even violence.

An Expanded View of Authority

Because they are dealing with a more dynamic and fluid organizational world characterized by the desire for more autonomy and self-management, GEMs need to develop a more robust sense of how authority is negotiated in organizations. In the previous chapter, we distinguished between *organizational* authority, the legitimate "right to work" within the boundaries of a defined role, and *personal* authority, or the "right to be" or to be one's own authentic self in any role, as a defining characteristic of a GEM. Such a manager comfortably inhabits the role of manager within a system, such as Executive VP, Department Head, or Chief Information Officer, and assumes all of the rights and responsibilities given to that role. At the same time the GEM understands and expresses his own vitality, passions, and creativity and readily accepts the same of others in executing that role.

GEMs give themselves and others permission to act autonomously and authentically and are not threatened by another's expressions of emotions or creativity. This orientation goes beyond typical definitions of "empowerment" where the one in power simply hands a bit over to one who has less, or, as Daniel Pink wryly puts it, "benevolently ladles some of it into the waiting bowls of grateful employees."[27] By exercising and encouraging personal authority, the manager accepts the power and vitality of others as an essential part of his own experience.[28] Such an expanded view of authority enables a manager to negotiate degrees of autonomy, accept strong emotions such as exuberance and anger without being overwhelmed or destroyed, and, when necessary, call a poor performer on the carpet and hold him accountable for his actions without blaming or apologizing.

Creating Learning Spaces

With the above-noted call for an open and interpretive approach, one of the tasks of a manager as teacher is to create a space for learning and creativity. It can be a physical space such as a conference room or even a virtual space facilitated by technology. Whatever form it takes, most importantly, it is a *psychological* space where imagination meets the demands of the environment or reality. Thinking back to John Keats's idea of negative capability, GEMs have this ability to create an intermediate space that enables them to continue to think through difficult situations and allow for the emergence of insight.[29] By providing a facilitating environment, a GEM also enables his employees to use their imaginations in the same way that a good enough mother provides the space for her growing child to engage in imaginative and productive play. Winnicott referred to this as a *potential* space where creativity and other forms of play, such as humor, are freely practiced.[30]

It is also useful to create spaces that allow for the development of effective interpersonal relations. In their landmark book, *In Search of Excellence*, Tom Peters and Robert Waterman introduced the concept of Management by Walking Around, then practiced in firms such as United Airlines and Hewlett-Packard.[31] The idea was for the manager to get out of his office and interact with the employees who are actually doing the work of the company. It was such a simple yet radical idea in 1982, before hierarchies became more fluid and organizational authority was more collaboratively exercised. Managerial presence is crucial, although from what we have learned about micromanaging, there is a difference between walking around and just plain annoying people ("He's in the building!"). When the micro-managing boss visits, everyone looks busy and there are compliant smiles all around. Employees can sense genuine curiosity and a desire for feedback and concerns; they can also sense meddling. It is a crucial balancing act requiring presence, empathy, and non-intrusive respect for the work and ideas of others.

In a time when so much of communication is electronic and less personal, it is even more crucial to provide mechanisms, both structural and interpersonal, for managers and employees to get to know one another. One noteworthy technique is the process of New Leader Transition practiced at Hard Rock International through their "School of Hard Rocks." Adapted from the US Army, this exercise is designed to get to know the leader, shorten start-up time, prevent early problems, and help employees learn the style of the leader. While the leader is out of the room, the employees (or team) develop a series of questions that are carefully recorded and prioritized. The questions focus on several key areas: management style (frequency of interaction, basic style of operating); performance (expectations and measurement); decision-making (how much involvement, feedback); personal style (emotional hot buttons, how to react); existing business (specific issues and opportunities); and general information (personal information such as interests outside of work, family). The leader is brought back and a chosen mediator presents the questions and the leader responds. Obviously, there are many variations of such a task, but the result is that a space is created for a productive and candid discussion that goes well beyond a basic orientation.[32]

A second technique that can prove useful in fostering ongoing relationships is the one-on-one meeting. Dean Smith, the renowned basketball coach of the University of North Carolina for 36 years, documents the way he interacted with players as a teacher and mentor as well as coach. He scheduled one-on-one meetings with each player at regular intervals: upon arrival on campus, at the start of practice, after the first scrimmage, and then several times during the season to go over films and check on their lives as students. In addition to honing skills on the court, Coach Smith was able to address larger problems with academic or personal life and provide for the inevitable "teachable moments." As a result, even in retirement, Smith enjoys life-long relationships with superstars such as Michael Jordan as well as those players who chose other life paths beyond basketball. By carving out such a learning space, any manager can provide the opportunity to discuss employee needs, ideas, and problems and set the stage for true mentoring.[33]

Lessons for GEMs

1   As a manager, embrace the role of teacher, who releases the creative capacity of others and guides their efforts toward goals.
2   Position yourself at the boundary between knowing and not knowing, a part of, yet apart from the working group. Let go of your natural desire to jump into the fray. Hover as a knowledgeable and authoritative presence, but don't intrude.
3   Serve as an interpreter, a conductor of ideas, emotions, and experiences.
4   Put your empathy, curiosity, and personal authority to work.

Competence

A particular value of emotional intelligence (or EQ) is the idea that specific emotional competencies can be learned and developed over time. I have devoted the better part of my academic career to the teaching of "Interpersonal Relations in Management," a course that emphasizes both capacity as discussed above and several clusters of interpersonal skills. The primary focus is on the competencies of: listening, assertive expression, and constructive approaches to conflict and confrontation. The stories about the best and worst managers also emphasized such concrete skills as listening and the ability to communicate clearly and effectively, particularly as regards the giving of performance feedback. While it is not a comprehensive program (there are plenty of texts and training programs available to enhance a variety of skills), this part of the discussion will highlight how a manager can begin to develop and enhance these skills, with an emphasis on how these skills build on the foundation provided by the empathic facilitating environment that is characteristic of GEMs.

Listening

Perhaps nowhere in the behavioral repertoire of a good enough manager is there a more salient interpersonal skill than listening. It is through listening in adult life that the echoes of the earliest relationship between mother and child can be heard and experienced. The human desire to be recognized, acknowledged, heard, and understood radiates from that primal interaction, and sets the stage for effective interpersonal relationships in both personal and work settings. It is here that a child sees himself in his mother's reflective gaze as she "mirrors" his experiences, including a full spectrum of emotions; it is here that the child comes to understand that he is a unique and separate individual who can engage in a productive exchange with another person. Through displays of empathy in her attempts to understand and appreciate her child's inner experience, the good enough mother provides the holding environment that contains the child's natural aggression, and expressions of frustration and joy. Although much of this primal exchange is unconscious and largely nonverbal, it is continually re-experienced in later settings as an individual interacts with many other authority figures, including teachers and managers, and the vestiges of these earlier experiences are activated.

While it is beyond the scope of this discussion to engage in a full discourse on human development, it is important for managers to recognize the power of their role as an engaged and responsive presence in interacting with their employees, co-workers, and other constituents in the larger system. Careful and precise listening provides the basis for building trust, communicating respect, and developing meaningful interactions and productive work relationships. It is the first step in approaching problems, generating new and creative ideas, responding to employee concerns, and making the most of teachable moments. Also, in our hyperactive 24/7 world of texts and tweets, actually paying attention to someone for more than a few moments can prove both refreshing and nourishing. Younger people, especially those of the emerging millennial generation, are not as used to communicating face-to-face and may even find it intimidating and too intense. Managers may wish to temper their efforts accordingly, by making interactions shorter and more casual. I have found, however, that this age cohort eventually finds substantive, one-on-one exchanges even more valuable because it is an increasingly rare experience.

Effective listening begins with the understanding and appreciation of the importance of the manager as teacher/counselor/coach/mentor. That multifaceted role has been previously revealed and reinforced in the study and discussion. It is in the listening setting that this important role is directly put into practice. Most guides to listening start with the realization that *listening is more attitude than skill*. Anyone can learn mechanical skills and try to repro-

duce a scripted response in the form of "I know how you feel" or "You feel
_____ because_____." The recipients of such well-intended efforts may appreciate the attempt, but if they do not perceive the attitude of empathy,
acceptance, and genuine concern behind the words, the exchange will ring
hollow. We recognize that capacity in the form of empathy and emotional
authenticity, and competence in the form of concrete skills, are vitally
interconnected.

We can amend our previous learning assumption and state that *effective
listening occurs at the edge between knowing and not knowing.* True listening
places managers on that boundary, with the understanding that they have a
base of knowledge and experience, and their own frame of reference that is
brought to every encounter. At the same time we employ empathy and curiosity to reach into the world of another person that we ultimately do not
know. That is why well-intended words such as "I know exactly how you
feel" don't ring true because the other person often responds with an unspoken but heartfelt "No, actually you don't." We spend so much of our time in
the daily give-and-take of email and text exchanges, and the small talk that
can serve as the lubricant for pleasant relationships on the surface. Such
cocktail party listening usually amounts to, in effect, "hello, I superficially
acknowledge your existence" and invites a similar mundane response in
return. I do not belittle these exchanges because they can serve the larger
purpose of greasing the social wheels, but these kinds of exchanges must also
be accompanied by deeper discussions that go beyond the usual back and
forth banter of friendly office relationships.

That is why Steven Covey, in discussing listening as one of his seven
habits, observed that most of us are not used to listening for understanding;
rather, we mainly listen in order to reply. We are already formulating our
response before the other person has fully expressed his idea or concern. This
is why a lot of "listening" takes the form of "yes, but don't you really
think..." (turning the exchange into a debate with a rebuttal) or "that happened to me once, too ..." (launching into the listener's own story that may
or may not be relevant), or worse, "you think that's bad..." (trying to one-up
the speaker often with the consequence of minimizing or devaluing the
speaker's experience). It thus becomes of critical importance to listen first
(and fully) and then respond, or as Covey put it: seek first to understand and
then to be understood.[34]

How one actually does this in practice presents a challenge. We begin by
going back to the primal relationship and understand that in a listening
situation *the manager is the mirror.* Carved into the proscenium above the
stage of the Huntington Theater in Boston is Shakespeare's observation
expressed through Hamlet: "to hold as 'twere a mirror to nature," the infer-
ence being that the theater enables us to see ourselves as we engage with the
action on the stage. Being a mirror means reflecting experience back to

another person in a process known as *reflective listening*. As mirroring reinforces a child's unique experience and enables autonomy in relation to another person (initially, his mother), reflecting is a major skill of a GEM that can reinforce an employee's right to have a struggle and then to express ideas and feelings facilitated by the GEM's active and engaged presence. It is a form of listening that is set in motion and best practiced when the manager is cast into a "helping" or counseling role, as when an employee or fellow co-worker presents a problem or concern or needs "advice."

A word of caution here: just because someone asks for advice doesn't necessarily mean that he wants direct advice ... at least not right away. In our business cultures where having a problem may be perceived as a vulnerability or even a weakness, we do not have precise language that says, in effect, "I'm having some difficulty with a situation. Could you please help me by listening to me for a moment?" Also, as the study suggests, many of these cultures are male-oriented cultures and males tend to like to solve problems by giving advice. Think of advice as a code word for active and reflective listening that may eventually lead to offering a perspective or even some helpful and relevant courses of action. Sometimes the speaker already knows what he wants to do and simply needs the permission and platform to say it out loud. It is helpful here to understand that people are walking narratives, and your purpose is to encourage the speaker to tell his story.

Once you are in the helping role, it is most important to create a space for listening, in this case a space defined by a specific time and place. If it is urgent, you can respond immediately, but even in the moment, make sure to respect the other person's privacy and seek a place out of the public arena such as an office or conference room. Otherwise, set up a mutually agreeable appointment and be mindful of respecting your time and the other person's time, and the significance of the place. The manager's office may be intimidating and get in the way of a meaningful exchange, although some offices have a space for such conversations that tend to level the playing field. Or, find a neutral spot. It is crucial to give the person your undivided attention, communicated by refraining from our usual habits of multi-tasking. Do not let phonecalls, emails or other interruptions get in the way. Make sure the person is as comfortable as possible, knowing that he may feel vulnerable and anxious, or even agitated depending on the situation that brings him to you. Once the stage is set, you as the manager may warm things up a bit with some casual small talk and then initiate the conversation by asking an open-ended question (in your own vernacular) to the effect of "What's happening?" or "How might I be of assistance?" or simply confirm "You wanted to speak with me." As the frame is now set, it is time to let go and become a mirror while the employee begins his story.

As the story unfolds, you may now put into practice the main idea addressed earlier: don't just do something, sit there. But, sit there as an active and engaged presence, communicating this involvement by your verbal, and more importantly, your nonverbal responses, such as culturally appropriate eye contact and physical distance. You can employ several reflective listening skills that vary in depth and intensity. As the person speaks, focus on *non-verbal attending* that affirms your connection to the speaker. Lean a bit towards him, but do not intrude on his personal space. Make appropriate eye contact, but do not stare at him or make him feel like this is a deposition. Your role is to facilitate, to smooth the way so that he can say what is on his mind. Since it is likely that you may have a hunch or hypothesis about what is involved, keep an open mind as new information comes in.

It is most important to check your understanding to make sure you are "getting it." The timing of these interventions comes with practice, but at a particular point or pause you can reflect the content back to the speaker by *paraphrasing* or providing a brief summary of what you are understanding so far. These short statements or questions help confirm that the manager as a listener is comprehending the details of the story, to say in so many words.... "Let me see if I have what you are saying so far. You are saying _____. Is that right?" The speaker may respond with "Right" or even "Exactly!" or, if needed, "No, that's not quite it. It's actually _____ [and he will clarify the facts]." It is important to understand that paraphrasing is not repeating, as that would result in a very frustrating and ultimately unproductive conversation, not to mention the reaction of "I just said that" from the speaker. Paraphrasing sends the implicit message that you are putting empathy into action by demonstrating an active attempt to receive and understand the facts as they are experienced by the speaker.

As the narrative develops and the basis of understanding is established, you can also try listening for the meaning, in addition to the facts. The process of *reflecting meaning* or *interpreting* blends your developing thoughts and knowledge about the situation and ideas expressed, with the others' attempts to put it into words. You can think of it as listening to what is not being said, or "listening to what the person is trying to say and saying without trying."[35] The implied meaning may be revealed in body language, tone of voice, or simply a hypothesis that you can present in the same manner of a paraphrase. At a key moment, you may say something such as: "It sounds to me like_____" or "From what I have heard so far, you seem to have a few options: _____." Once again the speaker will either confirm your understanding, build upon it, or explain it in more depth in order to clarify it. As the other person hears his own words reflected by you he gains a better understanding of his own meaning and implications. It is a bit riskier than paraphrasing because you are venturing more into the unknown area, but the outcome can be very valuable.

Finally, the deepest form of listening occurs at the emotional level. By *reflecting feelings* you are truly empathizing with your employee as you respond to the emotions being expressed or implied in the narrative. It is important to try to name the feeling and to try to be precise in your attempt to understand the level and intensity. Disappointment in not getting a promotion is substantially different from being devastated by a loss. Irritated feels different from enraged. Apprehensive is different from terrified. It is here that you as the participant-observer can pay attention to your own emotional and physical sensations stimulated by the resonant empathy described earlier. Some simple emotional statements such as "How exciting!" or "I can imagine your frustration" can open the door to a very productive conversation because now facts and events are connected to the emotional reactions. As we know, emotions are data that can be understood, managed, and put to good use. Your job here is not to psychoanalyze or "cure" the speaker; it is simply to understand how he is feeling and how these feelings are coloring his view of a situation, his relationships with others, and ultimately his work.

One of the worst things to do is to try to rationalize or get him to stop feeling whatever it is he is feeling. "You're over-reacting" or "Don't be angry" have seldom proved useful responses and will likely make matters worse because now the person has at least two things to be angry about: whatever has made him angry, and your refusal to allow him the right to feel what he is feeling in that moment. In either case, the person will become defensive, you in turn will become defensive, and communication stops. Emotions do not turn on and off like a light switch. Rather, we feel them in a cycle that builds and then dissipates, like the shape of a bell curve. The size and shape of these cycles differ from person to person as some have a "short fuse," react quickly and then it's over, while others are on more of a slow burn, and it takes them longer to fully react. Getting to know your employees' patterns may help when it comes time to listen to them.

Effective listening requires a combination of these skills and, like other learned skills, their exercise does not feel comfortable right away. Think of the first time you drove a car or attempted to hit a golfball; with practice you eventually got a feel for the mechanical actions involved and could pay more attention to refining them. The same is true for listening as over time and with practice (and a few successes) it becomes part of your natural style of conversation. You are able to tolerate not knowing exactly where the conversation is going and can follow more than lead. You can also resist the temptation to immediately fill in a moment of silence because that pause may provide the space needed for a new idea or insight to develop. Listening can lead to more real dialogue as after you have heard and understood, you can provide some of your ideas, give some advice that is now more relevant and meaningful, provide a larger perspective, or, as we will soon see, even engage in productive debate.

Where's the Fire?

Each year millions of acres of forest land are destroyed by wildfires. The news footage of these disasters, mostly occuring in the American west, are very dramatic as the fires often threaten and at times even consume nearby homes. Although mostly caused by people, the fires are often naturally occurring phenomena caused by a combination of environmental conditions. Such fires are certainly threatening to people and property and make dramatic news footage; however, we often overlook their potential benefits. By burning dead or decaying vegetation and destroying harmful insects and disease, the fires return nutrients to the soil and serve as a natural disinfectant, ultimately resulting in a more healthy ecosystem. Also, they clear overgrown canopies and underbrush, enabling more sunlight to reach the forest floor so that new seedlings can grow.[36]

I present these ideas about a natural occurrence because fire can serve as a useful metaphor for interpersonal conflict in organizations. How many times have you heard an exasperated manager complain that she spent the whole day "putting out fires?" Conflict occurs when individual frames of reference clash, when people interpret the meaning of events differently or see a potential threat in the words or actions of another person. The release of emotions, such as frustration or anger as a result of these conditions, provide the fuel for these fires. Whenever I ask students or practicing managers to provide their instant associations to the word "conflict" the results have overwhelmingly negative connotations: fight, disagreement, hostility, discomfort, resentment. Occasionally, someone will see a potential benefit such as a clarification or opportunity, but these ideas are in the minority of responses. Yet, we must ask ourselves, are all conflicts bad? Do all fires and conflicts need to be extinguished?

Staying with the metaphor, we can understand that, like fire, conflict is either helpful or destructive depending on the circumstances. Fire is a source of energy that can give off both heat and light depending on how it is managed. I love a fire in a fireplace or a wood-burning stove as long as it stays in its designated place and does not jump its boundaries. I can even add some fuel to turn up the heat as long as it is ventilated and properly tended. Such fireplaces usually add value to a home even if not the sole source of heat.

An intense brushfire can spread because it is still burning underground and can travel and flare up in another location even if nothing appears to be burning on the surface. Likewise, a manager may think she squelched a conflict only to see it "reignite" because the root causes were not addressed. The manager has to look at both sides of a conflict and decide if this particular conflict needs to be immediately resolved or if it can burn for a while to allow potential benefits, such as creative ideas, to emerge. The most important aspect for the manager is *containment*, making sure to manage the boundaries of the conflict so that the fire does not get out of hand. This means finding effective ways to mediate, listening carefully to both sides, and constructively confronting when necessary.

Constructive Confrontation

Most people find confronting another person threatening and avoid or resist it at all costs. And the costs can be high, especially if someone is doing something or acting in a way that is either annoying, destructive or, at the very least, unproductive or distracting to the task. We hope that it (or he or she) will either go away (a form of denial) or that by dropping subtle hints (usually too subtle for the other person to comprehend), he will stop the behavior (wishful thinking). The line of reasoning goes something like this: if I leave my stuff all over his work station like he does, he will find it annoying, realize his bad behavior and stop. Most times the other person will just wonder why I can't clean up after myself and make no connection to his own behavior. And why should he? I haven't made the connection between desired behavior and outcomes. But if I somehow think this person "should" know, I may then harbor resentment because he just doesn't see the value in my lesson. I can even make matters worse and act on this resentment by withholding my attention (the silent treatment) and let my resentment build like a savings account. Over time, my account collects compounded daily interest until it explodes into a needless fight that can leave much destruction in its wake that is difficult to repair.[37] It also can create a toxic undercurrent because this is what most people fear about confrontation: it will inevitably lead to something destructive. I fear that my aggressive impulses will hurt someone or I fear the other's aggression in the form of retaliation and end up getting hurt myself. I therefore say nothing and let the moment pass, but the feelings do not pass. If you find yourself having imaginary conversations while driving home or recounting your outrage to anyone who will listen, then avoidance was probably not the best solution.

It need not be this way. Successful confrontation comes under the general heading of assertive behavior, the positive aspect of our natural aggression. We need aggression to survive and to perform our work, but we also fear our own aggression as well as that of others, often for good reasons. Overly aggressive behavior stems from a desire to win at all costs and make sure the other person loses. One may seek to destroy the other person's ideas or even commit destruction through violence. Assertive behavior, by contrast, is grounded on the general principle of acting in one's best interest by also taking the other into account. The purpose is to inform rather than to attack. Because the feelings of others are brought into consideration, assertiveness requires a kind of empathy. The goal is to preserve a relationship while getting one's point across, standing up for beliefs and expressing ideas and feelings.

The mathematical axiom of "the shortest distance between two points is a straight line" serves as the guide for the straightforward communication needed for successfully confronting another person. If I hold an attitude of preserving the relationship by helping the other person see his behavior and its consequences, I translate this into words by creating what communication expert Robert Bolton calls a *three-part assertive message*.[38] I focus on the *specific behavior* and not the person ("You arrived at the meeting 10 minutes late" rather than "why can't you ever arrive on time?" or worse, "you're so unreliable"). I also communicate how this behavior made me feel (I was "frustrated" or "irritated" or "disappointed"). It is important to communicate what you actually feel or felt, and the use of the word "I" reinforces the personal impact. I then link the behavior to the *consequences* for the larger system ("We couldn't start the next phase because you had the data we needed to begin the discussion"). This connection between behavior and outcomes forms the "so that" moment of holding someone accountable for results ("I need you to be on time with your report *so that* we have enough time to review the data before sending it to the auditors").[39]

One does not have to speak in such a stilted manner, and the message is best when translated into one's own way of speaking, but the three essential elements (specific behavior, feelings, and consequences) should be included in the confrontation message. It is important to be very specific about the behavior. If I merely say that someone was "rude" at a meeting, his/her first reaction will be to ask "how? when?" or "what did I do?" "what do you mean 'rude'?!" sparking a defensive reaction and a potentially distracting argument about the meaning of "rude." If I provide the "how" and "when" in the confrontation, the other person may still be somewhat defensive, but will not feel as personally attacked and may be more able to hear the real message, even if he doesn't like it. It is helpful to stay away from labels such as "rude" or "lazy" or "stupid" and focus on what actually happened as you saw it. It is also helpful to confront as soon after the incident as possible unless you are so enraged that a little time to cool off before saying something might be the best idea. Remember, impulse control is very helpful here. It is key to remember that the confrontation may be the beginning of a dialogue (not necessarily an argument or fight), and it is important to carefully and reflectively listen to the other side as the other party may well have a different take on the situation. Successful confrontation means that one says what must be said, when it must be said, and in the way it must be said without hedging or apologizing, and accomplish all this while preserving the relationship. It is also important that your body language, tone, and facial expressions reinforce your message. Your intent is to make your point *and* keep the relationship intact.

This form of behavior works best in managing difficult situations and in providing both constructive and useful performance feedback. This particular skill emerged with considerable frequency in the study as a feature that distinguished the best from worst managers. Feeback that enables an employee to learn and grow on the job is crucial to the teaching and mentoring role. It is best delivered as a natural extension of a trusting and respectful working relationship, yet one in which both parties are held accountable for performance in their respective roles. The GEM is open to receiving feedback as a part of giving it, whether as part of a formal performance review or an impromptu coaching or counseling session about a particular issue that has arisen. Like listening, these skills develop with practice and most guides to feedback focus on the key factors of being very specific and factual about the behavior and linking it to the impact (behavioral and emotional) on yourself, and the consequences for the larger group or organization. Bringing specific behavior and its consequences to the attention of an employee increases the likelihood that the person can actually do something about it. You can continue the teaching role by providing some helpful suggestions for next time and then use that as a basis for following up.

It is also important to note that assertive communication need not only apply to something negative and can also be the basis for positive reinforcement. ("Your comments at the meeting on Tuesday, especially your suggestions for cost savings, were right on target. Three people commented to me about how productive the meeting was and it was largely due to your careful assessments.") Getting through a conflict, hashing out the varying perspectives and containing the emotions, can reveal hidden concerns and fears, and also build respect and trust.

In examining all of the above competencies, one aspect shines through: these interactions are carried out *in person*. Given the world of instant communication and social media, it is very tempting to just send an email, fire off a text message, or even post something on Facebook. Modern managers have so many choices and determining the best form of communication is an art in itself. Marshall McLuhan famously observed, "the medium is the message" and employees and co-workers will be affected by the form as well as the content of the interaction.[40] What does it feel like to get feedback in an email? Can you effectively listen to someone electronically when so much of the power of the encounter is derived from nonverbal cues (still estimated to be the source of between 60 and 80 percent of total meaning)? The entire "good enough" approach is based on the primal mother–child interaction that is largely nonverbal, and the face-to-face encounter recapitulates the emotional power of this early relationship. Electonically mediated communication, while efficient, is not necessarily effective, although newer forms such as Skype and video streaming provide more opportunity to experience nonverbal interactions such as facial expressions. The difference is that between text and *context*.[41] An electronic message can, however, provide a useful way to follow up and summarize a feedback session. It also provides a written record for future documentation if necessary.

Enhancing Skills Through Continuous Learning

Because these skills are not always taught in business schools and do not come naturally to many managers, especially those who are promoted because of their technical success, it is important to find a way to learn and practice them. One useful and increasingly important avenue is executive coaching. This sub-area of consulting has exploded in the last 20 years as an outgrowth of organizational development, corporate assessment centers, executive education programs, feedback mechanisms, and the proliferation of behavioral therapy techniques.[42] The coaching relationship is more one-on-one, a helping relationship between a client and a consultant who uses a variety of techniques to improve performance and achieve mutually agreed upon goals.

In working with emotional intelligence skills such as listening and assertive expression, it is important to begin with diagnosis. When working with a client, a coach may make use of a variety of assessment instruments such as the Bar-On Emotional Quotient Inventory (EQi), the Hay Group's Emotional Competence Inventory (ECI), or the Mayer Salovey Caruso Emotional Intelligence Test (MSCEIT). Each of these instruments offers its own conceptual and applied approach to measuring emotional intelligence, and the scales and profiles are highly useful as a snapshot of current emotional functioning. They can be combined with other data such as 360-degree feedback and organizational interviews to get an accurate sense of general themes and particular areas that the manager needs to work on. The real value of these measures emerges from the interaction between the consultant and client and how the client learns about the meaning of the data in relation to his situation. The results are best seen as the beginning of an ongoing conversation where the client can discuss the meaning of the measures and jointly establish goals. The client can practice specific skills with the coach (as the coach becomes mentor and teacher) and learn to be more reflective in the managerial role.[43]

The value of such an approach became evident when I was engaged as a consultant to work with a senior manager of a large social service agency. The client was a middle-aged woman who was a development officer. Although she was an experienced and accomplished fundraiser, she was having some difficulty managing the stresses associated with being in charge of a large unit in an organization that was undergoing considerable structural and personnel changes. Having administered the EQi and conducted several interviews with colleagues, the results reinforced the idea that she needed to work on being more flexible and adaptable to changing circumstances, and more effective in presenting her ideas assertively and effectively, particularly to peers and upper management. We spent some time working on these and other skills, thinking through and planning for upcoming events, and working around some of the emotional strain of feeling short-staffed due to a combination of employee medical leaves and vacations at a crucial time. As she was preparing for her own vacation, we made sure that she was planning accordingly.

As we were discussing her vacation plans, she mentioned in passing how she had to gear up for going sailing with her husband, since sailing was not always a comfortable experience for her. Sensing an opportunity, I asked her if she saw any connections between sailing and her currrent management situation, and this thinking created a very important metaphor for her experience. As we thought through the parallel experiences, she explained that she coped by: packing well (planning and preparation), taking good physical care (getting enough sleep and eating properly, including bringing along crackers and ginger beer for seasickness), paying more careful attention (becoming highly focused on the immediate task), keeping sight of land (being mindful of larger goals and seeking safety), taking on the role of navigator (tracking measurements related to goals), emphasizing the positive (such as the beautiful weather), and looking at the overall patterns and rhythms (vision and strategy amid changing circumstances). It was an eye-opening and mind-opening moment of insight. Although she left the agency a few months later for a similar job in another type of organization, the sailing metaphor stayed with her as a way to reflect on her role as a manager.

Lessons for GEMs

1 The skills of reflective listening and constructive confrontation are your instruments, as a mentor and teacher to release the potential of your employees.
2 Conflict, like fire, can either be a destructive force or, when managed and contained, a source of inspiration.
3 Both sets of skills build on a foundation of empathy and can be practiced and honed over time to provide the mirroring experience along with open and clear communication.
4 The skills need to be the basis for continued practice and learning.

Character

I often pose the following questions to students: what kind of manager do you want to be? What kind of person do you want to be? What do you want your legacy to be? Managing is not just about business; it's also about how you go about your business. The study revealed that the best managers had their eye on their moral compass as well as the task. There is another mirror that must be considered and that is the one we hold up to ourselves. In the last 40 years it seems that we have come to a reckoning, especially after spectacular moral lapses such as the network of politically corrupt events collectively known as Watergate, the savings and loan scandal of the 1980s, the collapse of once-heralded giants such as Enron and WorldCom in the late 1990s and early 2000s, and the Madoff scandal and recent financial debacle with aftershocks still rumbling throughout the world economy. We gasp at the excesses and the triumph of greed over ethics. There are calls for investigations and exhortations of the need for ethics in business education to counter the perceived amorality of business executives. It's a familiar call, somewhat like rounding up the usual suspects.

Beyond political solutions in the form of tighter regulations, some students and faculty at elite educational institutions have proposed larger and more direct measures, such as an ethical oath for business leaders similar to the Hippocratic oath for the medical profession.[44] Proponents of the oath cite examples of swearing on the Bible and other public declarations that cognitive dissonance researchers have shown increase private adherence to the stated values. Critics of such a plan question whether business is actually a profession with a higher purpose beyond maximizing profit and shareholder value, and point to the idea that an oath ignores inevitable compromises and tradeoffs, and their value implications.

Since the GEMs seemed to operate according to a clearer sense of their values, as shown in the previous chapter, it is important for managers to engage in the kind of introspection that leads to the clarification of these values. There is a growing body of research evidence that suggests that our moral sense forms much earlier in life than previously assumed, and although culture still plays a strong role in the formation of values, babies under the age of two can display a rudimentary form of empathy and compassion. Such evolutionary claims to a primitive morality pose important challenges as we explore how managers make decisions and treat their employees. Yale psychologist Paul Bloom, whose research focuses of the early development of morality, proposes that the core principle of mature morality is *impartiality*, a concept that underlies our larger ideas of justice and the rule of law, and by extension, fair and effective managing. Remember, the GEMs were heralded for not playing favorites and not taking credit for others' accomplishments. We start off with this very basic moral sense that provides a foundation for elaboration through family and cultural influences on our growth and development. Bloom concludes:

> Morality, then, is a synthesis of the biological and the cultural, of the unlearned, the discovered and the invented. Babies possess certain

moral foundations – the capacity and willingness to judge the actions of others, some sense of justice, gut responses to altruism and nastiness. Regardless of how smart we are, if we didn't start with this basic apparatus, we would be nothing more than amoral agents, ruthlessly driven to pursue our self-interest. But our capacities as babies are sharply limited. It is the insights of rational individuals that make a truly universal and unselfish morality something that our species can aspire to.[45]

Values in Action

However they are determined, we can see this moral foundation play out in very familiar circumstances, including that most American of venues, the baseball diamond. On May 26, 2010, Detroit Tigers pitcher Armando Galarraga was one out shy of a perfect game, when the twenty-seventh and last hitter, Jason Donald, hit a ground ball that seemed like a sure final out and the entry of the twenty-first perfect game into the record books and baseball history. The ball was easily scooped up by the first baseman and tossed to the pitcher, Galarraga, in what seemed plenty of time. Yet, to the shock of all, the umpire, Jim Joyce, called the runner safe and the perfect game evaporated in that stunning moment. Replays clearly showed that the throw was there in time, and during the next few days there were pleas to the Commissioner of Baseball to reverse the call, but he refused to intervene and the decision stood.

It was a heartbreaking loss; however, something more important and fundamental occurred. The umpire, Joyce, actually admitted that he made a mistake and immediately (and emotionally) apologized to Galarraga, who responded with a magnanimity that few could comprehend: nobody's perfect, we all make mistakes. No bravado, no defensiveness, no threatened lawsuits or aggrieved appearance on a talk show, and the world seemed amazed and awed by the show of class and grace on the part of both men. Galarraga was even awarded a car by General Motors as a kind of consolation prize.[46] Perhaps the real prize was something that the larger culture gained from this episode as it unfolded as a kind of morality play.

It's only the game of baseball, but this was another teachable moment. How can we gain more access to the kind of moral foundation that led to such a positive outcome from a flawed decision? A predominant theme underlying the good enough manager is "nobody's perfect" and there is much to gain from appreciating the value inherent in comprehending and admitting imperfection. We don't hear much about personal virtues such as humility, grace under pressure, and the kinds of behavior that get labelled "class" in business practice these days. Yet these were major components of the perceptions of the best managers, such as Tom in Chapter 5.

It is important to note that, like all systems, this value substrata is inextricably connected to a larger environment. Social psychology informs us that although the basics of value formation may be ingrained in the individual, their shape and structure is socially influenced. As Kurt Lewin famously stated, behavior is the result of an interaction between the individual and the environment.[47] We all come under the powerful influences of our families, friends, cultures, religions, educational practices, and larger political and economic forces. To make matters even more complex, we seek cognitive consistency and are more "rationalizing" than rational creatures. Behavior that deviates from our deeply held individual values (such as honesty or loyalty) causes dissonance and tension that we seek to reduce by altering our perceptions in an attempt to justify and even distort the behavior to bring it into line with our values ("everyone does it," "he deserved it").[48] We are constantly calibrating our behavior with our deeply held values.

Illuminating One's Values

There are numerous "values clarification" exercises that are a staple of training and development seminars and organizational behavior classes. The exercises usually begin with participants generating a series of "value lists" (such as achievement, recognition, justice, love, freedom, etc.) followed by a winnowing and sorting process until a set of prioritized core values is identified. The protocol may follow different classifications such as intrinsic and extrinsic or personal and professional and then linked either to important people (role models) or current challenges. Other exercises might involve survivors on a lifeboat or a reaction to a value-laden parable. Each has its merit as long as the value implications are explored. One particularly powerful exercise is based on our view of ourselves in important roles and proceeds as follows:

1   List at least five different roles that you inhabit in your life (consider items such as son, student, wife, vice president, volunteer leader).
2   For each role identify the tasks, relationships and emotions associated with the role.
3   For external reasons, you are now asked to relinquish one of the roles. Which one would you eliminate first, knowing that you are also forsaking all that goes with it?
4   As you examine your remaining roles, you are now asked to relinquish another role. Which one would be the next?
5   The process continues with each succeeding role.

As you might predict, there comes a point when participants find this extremely difficult as the losses implied with the elimination of each remaining role become emotionally unbearable, even in the hypothetical case. One does end up with more clarity about life priorities and how these can influence decisions and behavior.

Another way to approach values and their implications is to project into the future and describe yourself in the ideal, drawing upon ideas about the "ego ideal" or our vision of ourselves at our "future best."[49] Once this description is completed in detail, you can compare it with your current reality or the "self image" and note how close or far apart these two sets of ideas are. You can then translate these ideals into a list of your guiding *assumptions* or personal rules or "shoulds" about various issues, such as how to treat employees, make a decision, or deal with a conflict.[50] We often do not realize the power of these assumptions until one or more of them are violated, triggering an emotional response such as anger or betrayal. However they are determined, it is important to be specific about the values that are central to our social fabric.

Personal Narratives

It is often said that we live our lives forward and understand them backward. We tend to condense our lives into a coherent narrative that can reveal emergent truths in retrospect. We can see the interdependent events and relationships that ultimately shaped our worldview. Our values can be revealed as they are evolved from "watershed" moments formed by events of particular emotional magnitude. We can identify the mentors and teachers that we have continually sought to emulate, and learn how important values were transmuted and internalized at crucial moments.

As an illustration, let me share one such moment that stands out for me. My father died suddenly when I was a 19-year-old college sophomore. It was an unexpected tragedy for my entire family that had many ripple effects for years to come. I was raised in a small southern town in the pre-Civil Rights south. Although my father's death happened in 1971, a full five years after the Civil Rights legislation of the mid 1960s, the town was only beginning to emerge from the longstanding and entrenched cultural traditions of segregation. As is typical of small town life, over the course of several days many townspeople came to pay their respects to my family, especially to my uncle, who in his grief recounted the story of my father's passing to friends, neighbors, and customers of many years. In the midst of one of these visits, I watched as a sedan pulled in front of our house and a prominent black minister and his family approached our door. My uncle greeted him and invited him in. "The preacher," as my uncle called him, was very formally dressed in a black suit and he immediately sought me out. As he extended his hand and looked me in the eye, he said very quietly and proudly, "Your Daddy sold me this suit."

I didn't think much of it beyond his gentle kindness and grace at the time, but the minister's remark stayed with me. In my adult years, I was reminded of the powerful scene in *To Kill a Mockingbird* when the black community, seated in the rafters of the hot courthouse, quietly and reverently stood as Atticus Finch, who had just (unsuccessfully) defended Tom Robinson, a black man falsely accused of rape, calmly packed up his papers and left the courtroom. Let's be clear: my father was no Atticus Finch, and he certainly would not have qualified as a civil rights activist. But, in a time when black men in our town could not enter many business establishments, much less buy a suit, the minister had obviously been welcomed in our store many times, and the subtext of his kind gesture spoke volumes.

I remember, now with greater context and perspective, how I was taught as a child by my father and uncle that every customer was to be treated with respect and they showed me how to greet them in "rehearsals." It was a powerful transmission of values: that such an approach not only was the right thing to do, it was also a good business practice; and it resulted in strong customer loyalty that was beautifully expressed to me at a crucial time. Many years later, I was invited by a female African American colleague to conduct diversity workshops (billed as sensitivity training) to some challenging and, at times, outright hostile audiences. Part of our training sessions involved the telling of personal stories about race, in an attempt to make "the undiscussable, discussable." The personal storytelling often had much more effect than abstract theories and guidelines, and several of our more resistant participants eventually came around and even offered stories of their own.

Valuing Differences

Speaking of diversity, it is now common knowledge that the workforce has changed dramatically in the last 30 years with more traditionally under-represented groups having a greater presence and impact. Given changing demographic patterns, it is much more likely that a manager will be working across and among differences in race, ethnicity, gender, religion, and sexual orientation, and the likelihood of making a mistake such as stereotyping, inadvertently insulting someone, or other faux pas increases. Although well-intended, often the fear of being labeled racist, sexist or homophobic has led to "politically correct" (or PC) cultures where "unspoken canons of propriety govern behavior in cross-cultural interactions."[51] While the idea underlying politically correct behavior, that is, to create a more inclusive experience for under-represented employees, the behavior itself can unfortunately create a restrictive and fearful environment, as well as suspicion and resentment in the majority population. The ultimate impact is that minorities suffer also because nobody feels free to speak openly about sensitive issues or give valuable and instructive feedback. Robin Ely and her associates recommend the following strategies for dealing with tensions related to the healthy management of differences:

- *Pause* to short-circuit the emotion and reflect.
- *Connect* with others in ways that affirm the importance of relationships.
- *Question yourself* to help identify your blind spots and discover what makes you defensive.
- *Get genuine support* that doesn't necessarily validate your point of view but, rather, helps you gain a better perspective.
- *Shift your mind-set* from "*You* need to change" to "What can *I* change?"[52]

Notice that these principles bear a striking resemblance to the behavior of GEMs discussed throughout this chapter: reflection, connection, questioning, seeking a larger view, and taking responsibility for one's behavior in relation to others.

Lessons for GEMS

1 We have a deeply held and ingrained sense of morality that is expanded and elaborated over time by external forces.
2 Values are often the product of deeds rather than words. While our values instruct us to do the right thing, we sometimes trip over our own behavior.
3 Virtues such as humility and grace can be powerful agents of effective management practice.
4 It is important to explore and clarify our most salient values through introspection, exercises, interactions with mentors, and personal narratives.

Commitment

With the fourth C, we move from an internal to more of an external focus. The GEMs were seen as appreciating interdependence, and the building and maintaining of effective relationships. They realized that good enough managing takes place in a social context and thus they are connected to something larger than themselves. We know that we are the product of individual and social forces and are part of complex interacting social systems and networks. The word *commitment* captures this more outward focus and the relationship between the *intra*-personal qualities of empathy and personal values to the *inter*-personal aspects of relationships and interactions with the larger community and environment. We can also learn that the connection between our individual passions to a larger and transcending purpose can give greater meaning to our work and the work of others.

Ethics and Social Responsibility

Business ethics and corporate social responsibility have become fixtures in business education during the last few decades and represent areas of study in and of themselves. One still hears jokes about the apparent oxymoron of "business ethics" as so much business behavior appears to be amoral if not immoral. There is an understanding and growing acceptance of the need for ethical practice in business, as represented by the rise of ethics officers and the development of elaborate and often legalistic ethical codes of conduct in companies and other organizations. Legislation, such as the Sarbanes-Oxley guidelines that emerged from the Enron era, reinforces social responsibility at the national level. From a more academic perspective, ethical reasoning is drawn from formal philosophical domains such as:

- ethical relativism – there are no universal standards for moral behavior;
- utilitarianism – actions are judged based on consequences;
- universalism – actions are based on an individual's duty to other individuals and humanity;
- rights and entitlements – life, liberty and the pursuit of happiness;
- justice – fairness and equality.

From any of these perspectives, ethical reasoning is applied to making moral judgments that seek to balance self-interest and the larger social good. Ethics are considered and practiced within a "stakeholder" framework rather than one that caters exclusively to stockholders. One can map and examine the primary and secondary stakeholders, defined as those who are affected by decisions, policies, or practices; these can include employees, customers, suppliers, political organizations, competitors, government, etc.[53] The key is understanding who the stakeholders are and how they are affected, with the ultimate goal of understanding tradeoffs and striving as much as possible for win-win relationships.

To get a sense of whether a given action or decision is deemed ethical, a manager might put it to the following simple test:

1   Is it right?
2   Is it fair?
3   Does someone get hurt, and if so, who?
4   Would you be comfortable if the details of the decision were reported on the front page of your local newspaper?
5   What would you tell your child to do?
6   Does it pass the "smell" test? How does it feel?[54]

We might expand the above questions to include electronic forms of communication and ask whether one is comfortable having information about the action forwarded to multiple distribution lists, escaping into the blogosphere, going viral, and ending up on the front page of major newspapers and discussed by pundits on CNN and Fox News.

As we learned earlier, emotions are data and the body does not lie. If it doesn't feel right "in your gut," then perhaps a second look is advisable. This might include a more nuanced consideration of the sources of dissonance and tension. Do you immediately seek to rationalize or justify the action? As Elliot Aronson states, "Man cannot live by consonance alone" and our first impulse when experiencing a clash between our behavior and our values is to seek to reduce the tension caused by the inner conflict by altering the competing thoughts and feelings by rationalizing or justifying the behavior. However, such a short-term strategy may not work in the long run, and it is more useful to live with the complexity of the decision and its implications for a while before taking quick actions that simply make one feel better. Aronson concludes that there are many ways to learn from inevitable mistakes and failures, and suggests the following pathways for gaining this kind of insight:

- Through a greater understanding of my own defensiveness and dissonance-reducing tendencies.
- Through the realization that performing stupid or immoral actions does not necessarily mean that I am an irrevocably stupid or immoral person.
- Through the development of enough ego strength to tolerate errors in myself.
- Through increasing my ability to recognize the benefits of admitting my errors in terms of my own growth and learning as well as my ability to form close, meaningful relationships with other people.[55]

We know that social responsibility is an important element of emotional intelligence. It is manifested by a person demonstrating that he is a cooperative, contributing, and constructive member of a social group. It involves accepting others, following one's conscience, and upholding social rules and taking into consideration the good of the community and not just the self.[56] To get a sense of one's own social responsibility, think of the network of overlapping groups to which you belong. Are any of these community organizations in which you volunteer? What is your role in each of these? How do you allocate your time and financial resources to charitable causes or events? How do you display your sensitivity to the needs of friends, acquaintances or co-workers? How is your behavior affected by its perceived impact on the larger community?[57]

A Larger Purpose

Beyond social responsibility is a commitment to a larger purpose in managing, something that provides greater meaning to one's life and reaching beyond increasing shareholder value and accumulating wealth. According to some observers, we have entered an age of "transcendence" in our society's cultural evolution. Fueled by such factors as increased longevity and the democratization of information on the Internet, people advancing through mid-life to more senior status are looking for greater meaning in life, more autonomy in decisions and self-expression through open forums and blogs, and a significant orientation toward the metaphysical and subjective experiences, including those involved with work. Quality of work life has now transcended into the larger realm of quality of one's *whole life* and a more "conscious" approach to capitalism. Companies such as Whole Foods, Trader Joe's, Zappos, Starbucks, and The Container Store are on the leading edge of this movement. Such humanistic companies

> Seek to maximize their value to society as a whole, not just their shareholders. They are the ultimate value creators: They create emotional value, experiential value, social value, and, of course, financial value. People who interact with such companies feel safe, secure, and pleased with their dealings. They enjoy working with or for the company, buying from it, investing in it, and having it as a neighbor.[58]

The above-noted companies combine the emotional with the operational and move from a stakeholder approach or analysis to active stakeholder relationship management. As Starbucks CEO Howard Schultz recently commented in describing his company projected 40 years into the future, "the core of our mission will still be about achieving that fragile balance between profitability and social conscience. Without the latter, the former is unsustainable."[59] The GEMs are ideally suited to manage in such a world as they bring their own emotional aptitude into their daily work and seek to interpret and negotiate meaning from experience and translate it to a larger, in this case societal, context.

Among these companies with a larger purpose, Zappos very carefully articulates a set of core values that seem to embrace an underlying GEM philosophy of work. Originally founded as an online shoe retailer, Zappos has joined with Amazon and has re-structured itself into ten companies under one umbrella to provide a complete range of products and services with a central emphasis on outstanding customer service and a unique company culture. The values that constitute that culture include the following:

1 Deliver WOW through service.

The family of companies seeks to differentiate itself through innovative and unconventional practices that impress customers, co-workers, vendors, partners and investors.

2 Embrace and drive change.

Change is viewed as a constant and a way to keep evolving and innovating.

3 Create fun and a little weirdness.

A conscious attempt to inject humor and individual personality into work encourages divergent thinking and creativity.

4 Be adventurous, creative, and open-minded.

The company encourages risk-taking that emphasizes using one's "gut" in decision-making and learning from mistakes.

5 Pursue growth and learning.

There is a built-in sense that the job is never done, they never fully get it right, and there is always a way to stretch abilities and seek new challenges.

6 Build open and honest relationships with communication.

The building of strong relationships and emotional bonds is highly encouraged. Words like "compassionate," "loyal", and "friendly" are specifically invoked to build trust and the company also emphasizes listening and communicating clearly.

7 Build a positive team and a family spirit.

There is an emphasis on servant leadership, removing obstacles to individual performance, and bottom-up communication.

8 Do more with less.

They focus on continuous operational improvement, setting high performance standards and efficiency.

9 Be passionate and determined.

Passion is considered contagious and leads to perseverance and a sense of urgency in work.

10 Be humble.

There is a belief in respect and quiet confidence; arrogance is specifically discouraged.

These core values appear, and are discussed in depth, on the Zappos website; they are constantly reinforced by CEO Tony Hseih, and could serve as a manifesto for good enough managing. As with other corporate leaders of this emerging generation, such as Howard Schultz of Starbucks and John Mackey of Whole Foods, the Zappos ideas are widely proliferated to the general public through social media, highly visible public appearances and events, and Hseih's book, *Delivering Happiness: A Path to Profits, Passion and Purpose.*[60]

What can aspiring GEMs learn from this conscious, value-based, neo-humanist approach to business? Think back to the ego ideal, the vision of yourself at your future best, and consider the following questions:

1 What is your highest purpose?
2 What activities, thoughts, and ideas bring the greatest meaning to your life?
3 What is your passion? What brings great joy to your life?
4 How can passion and purpose be infused into your daily life as a manager?

It is important to note that these ideals do not come to one immediately upon assuming a managerial role. I have often observed that in our digital world we often confuse information with knowledge, and knowledge with wisdom. Knowledge and wisdom evolve and emerge more at mid-life and beyond. Evoking T.H. White's *The Once and Future King*, Lawrence Gould concluded that knowledge of the world – that is, "the means by which men and women contrive to ride the waves of a world in which there is war, adultery, compromise, fear, stulfication, and hypocrisy"– is accompanied by a parallel knowledge of the self informed by the

> guilt, shame, and disappointment that one has not lived up to one's ideals. Such discovery and self-knowledge is also hardly an occasion for triumph, but if it leads, as it often does, to self-acceptance, it can be the basis for new possibilities of wholeness, vitality, and an emotionally rich and unconflicted sense of personal authority.[61]

In other words, the continuous quest for self-knowledge in relation to others in a larger context is the essence of becoming a good enough manager.

Lessons for GEMs

1 Managing requires a constant interplay between a manager's values and moral reasoning with an eye on stakeholders in the larger social context.
2 Social responsibility is a significant component of emotional intelligence and is crucial to being a productive and responsive organizational citizen.
3 Passion and purpose, along with persistence, hard work, and humility bring a greater sense of commitment to work and organizational life.

Appendix
Manager Survey Results

TABLE A.1. Manager Gender

		Count	Column N (%)
Best Manager Gender	Male	739	70.9
	Female	304	29.1
	Total	1,043	100.0
Worst Manager Gender	Male	654	63.6
	Female	374	36.4
	Total	1,028	100.0

TABLE A.2. Manager Gender by Respondent Gender

		Respondent Gender						
		Male		Female		Total		
		Count	Column N (%)	Count	Column N (%)	Count	Column N (%)	
Best Manager Gender	Male	451	84.6	281	56.2	732	70.9	
	Female	82	15.4	219	43.8	301	29.1	
	Total	533	100.0	500	100.0	1,033	100.0	
Worst Manager Gender	Male	386	73.2	265	53.2	651	63.5	
	Female	141	26.8	233	46.8	374	36.5	
	Total	527	100.0	498	100.0	1,025	100.0	

TABLE A.3. Years with Manager

	Mean
Years with Best Manager	3.73
Years with Worst Manager	2.72

TABLE A.4. Years with Manager by Respondent Gender

	Respondent Gender		
	Male Mean	Female Mean	Total Mean
Years with Best Manager	3.94	3.49	3.73
Years with Worst Manager	2.95	2.47	2.72

TABLE A.5. Years with Manager by Manager Gender

	Best Manager Gender			Worst Manager Gender		
	Male Mean	Female Mean	Total Mean	Male Mean	Female Mean	Total Mean
Years with Best Manager	3.91	3.23	3.72	3.85	3.47	3.71
Years with Worst Manager	2.77	2.53	2.70	2.84	2.45	2.70

TABLE A.6. Organization Type by Best Manager

| | Best Manager Gender | | | | | |
| | Male | | Female | | Total | |
	Count	Row N (%)	Count	Row N (%)	Count	Row N (%)
Financial	196	70.3	83	29.7	279	100.0
Public Accounting	58	80.6	14	19.4	72	100.0
Information Technology	93	72.1	36	27.9	129	100.0
Telecommunication	19	76.0	6	24.0	25	100.0
Industrial/Manufacturing	59	86.8	9	13.2	68	100.0
Consumer products	33	56.9	25	43.1	58	100.0
Health care/Medical	23	65.7	12	34.3	35	100.0
Energy	9	100.0	0	0.0	9	100.0
Scientific	4	80.0	1	20.0	5	100.0
Pharmaceutical/Biotechnology	11	73.3	4	26.7	15	100.0
Non-profit	14	46.7	16	53.3	30	100.0
Other	215	68.7	98	31.3	313	100.0
Total	734	70.7	304	29.3	1,038	100.0

TABLE A.7. Organization Type by Worst Manager

	Worst Manager Gender					
	Male		Female		Total	
	Count	Row N (%)	Count	Row N (%)	Count	Row N (%)
Financial	176	64.2	98	35.8	274	100.0
Public Accounting	54	71.1	22	28.9	76	100.0
Information Technology	77	65.3	41	34.7	118	100.0
Telecommunication	17	68.0	8	32.0	25	100.0
Industrial/Manufacturing	49	80.3	12	19.7	61	100.0
Consumer products	32	47.8	35	52.2	67	100.0
Health care/Medical	20	62.5	12	37.5	32	100.0
Energy	8	80.0	2	20.0	10	100.0
Scientific	2	50.0	2	50.0	4	100.0
Pharmaceutical/Biotechnology	10	58.8	7	41.2	17	100.0
Non-profit	13	41.9	18	58.1	31	100.0
Other	189	62.4	114	37.6	303	100.0
Total	647	63.6	371	36.4	1,018	100.0

TABLE A.8. Best Manager by Organization Type

| | Best Manager Gender | | | | | |
| | Male | | Female | | Total | |
	Count	Row N (%)	Count	Row N (%)	Count	Row N (%)
Financial	196	26.7	83	27.3	279	26.9
Public Accounting	58	7.9	14	4.6	72	6.9
Information Technology	93	12.7	36	11.8	129	12.4
Telecommunication	19	2.6	6	2.0	25	2.4
Industrial/Manufacturing	59	8.0	9	3.0	68	6.6
Consumer products	33	4.5	25	8.2	58	5.6
Health care/Medical	23	3.1	12	3.9	35	3.4
Energy	9	1.2	0	0.0	9	0.9
Scientific	4	0.5	1	0.3	5	0.5
Pharmaceutical/Biotechnology	11	1.5	4	1.3	15	1.4
Non-profit	14	1.9	16	5.3	30	2.9
Other	215	29.3	98	32.2	313	30.2
Total	734	100.0	304	100.0	1,038	100.0

TABLE A.9. Worst Manager by Organization Type

| | Worst Manager Gender | | | | | |
| | Male | | Female | | Total | |
	Count	Row N (%)	Count	Row N (%)	Count	Row N (%)
Financial	176	27.2	98	26.4	274	26.9
Public Accounting	54	8.3	22	5.9	76	7.5
Information Technology	77	11.9	41	11.1	118	11.6
Telecommunication	17	2.6	8	2.2	25	2.5
Industrial/Manufacturing	49	7.6	12	3.2	61	6.0
Consumer products	32	4.9	35	9.4	67	6.6
Health care/Medical	20	3.1	12	3.2	32	3.1
Energy	8	1.2	2	0.5	10	1.0
Scientific	2	0.3	2	0.5	4	0.4
Pharmaceutical/Biotechnology	10	1.5	7	1.9	17	1.7
Non-profit	13	2.0	18	4.9	31	3.0
Other	189	29.2	114	30.7	303	29.8
Total	647	100.0	371	100.0	1,018	100.0

TABLE A.10. Best Manager Themes by Gender of Manager

Mentor/Teacher

Female	Male	Total
97 (29.5%)	230 (69.9%)	329
31.9% total female	31.1% total male	
304 total female	739 total male	1,043*

Support

Female	Male	Total
50 (25.3%)	144 (72.7%)	198
16.2% total female	19.5% total male	
304 total female	739 total male	1,043

Autonomy (did not micro-manage)

Female	Male	Total
55 (30.2%)	126 (69.2%)	182
18.1% total female	17.1% total male	
304 total female	739 total male	1,043

Respect

Female	Male	Total
42 (29.2%)	102 (70.8%)	144
13.8% total female	13.8% total male	
304 total female	739 total male	1,043

Trustworthy

Female	Male	Total
37 (28%)	93 (70.5%)	132
12.2% total female	12.6% total male	
304 total female	739 total male	1,043

Listening

Female	Male	Total
32 (28.6%)	80 (71.4%)	112
10.5% total female	10.8% total male	
304 total female	739 total male	1,043

TABLE A.10. Continued

Open

Female	Male	Total
40 (37.7%)	65 (61.3%)	106
13.2% total female	8.8% total male	
304 total female	739 total male	1,043

Communication

Female	Male	Total
34 (32.7%)	70 (67.3%)	104
11.2% total female	9.5% total male	
304 total female	739 total male	1,043

Feedback

Female	Male	Total
36 (37.1%)	60 (61.9%)	97
11.8% total female	8.1% total male	
304 total female	739 total male	1,043

Fair

Female	Male	Total
17 (22.1%)	59 (76.6%)	77
5.6% total female	8.0% total male	
304 total female	739 total male	1,043

Honest

Female	Male	Total
16 (25.3%)	50 (73.5%)	68
5.3% total female	6.8% total male	
304 total female	739 total male	1,043

Relationship

Female	Male	Total
15 (30.6%)	34 (69.4%)	49
4.9% total female	4.6% total male	
304 total female	739 total male	1,043

Note
* 15 respondents did not indicate the gender of the best manager, reducing the number of cases to 1,043.

TABLE A.11. Worst Manager Themes by Gender of Manager
Micro-manager

Female	Male	Total
65 (39.6%)	98 (59.8%)	164
17.4% total female	15% total male	
304 total female	739 total male	1,043

Poor communication

Female	Male	Total
35 (33.7%)	69 (66.3%)	104
9.4% total female	10.6% total male	
304 total female	739 total male	1,043

Lack of respect

Female	Male	Total
34 (38.2%)	54 (60.7%)	89
9.1% total female	8.3% total male	
304 total female	739 total male	1,043

Takes credit

Female	Male	Total
26 (35.6%)	46 (63%)	73
7.0% total female	7.0% total male	
304 total female	739 total male	1,043

Lack of trust

Female	Male	Total
26 (37.1%)	43 (61.4%)	70
7.0% total female	6.6% total male	
304 total female	739 total male	1,043

Lack of feedback

Female	Male	Total
16 (28.6%)	40 (71.4%)	56
4.3% total female	6.1% total male	
304 total female	739 total male	1,043

continued

TABLE A.11. Continued
Condescending

Female	Male	Total
17 (34%)	32 (64%)	50
4.5% total female	4.9% total male	
304 total female	739 total male	1,043

Poor listening

Female	Male	Total
8 (17.4%)	38 (82.6%)	46
2.1% total female	5.8% total male	
304 total female	739 total male	1,043

Blame

Female	Male	Total
15 (41.7%)	21 (58.3%)	36
4% total female	3.2% total male	
304 total female	739 total male	1,043

Plays favorites

Female	Male	Total
14 (46.7%)	15 (50%)	30
3.7% total female	2.3% total male	
304 total female	739 total male	1,043

Insecure

Female	Male	Total
8 (33.3%)	16 (66.7%)	24
2.1% total female	2.4% total male	
304 total female	739 total male	1,043

Dishonest

Female	Male	Total
5 (27.8%)	12 (66.7%)	18
1.3% total female	1.8% total male	
304 total female	739 total male	1,043

TABLE A.11. Continued
Incompetent

Female	Male	Total
6 (50%)	6 (50%)	12
1.6% total female	0.9% total male	
304 total female	739 total male	1,043

Notes

1 Introduction: What is a "Good Enough" Manager?

1 Robert Sutton cites the work of James Meindl on the "romance of leadership" along with a Swedish study about the effects of managers on the incidence of cardiac illness in "Why Good Bosses Tune in to their People," *McKinsey Quarterly*, August, 2010. The emphasis of the person over environmental factors stems from the "fundamental attribution error" discussed in Elliot Aronson, *The Social Animal* (New York: Worth/Freeman, 2008).
2 Manfred Kets de Vries and Danny Miller, *The Neurotic Organization: Diagnosing and Changing Counterproductive Styles of Management* (San Francisco: Jossey-Bass, 1984).
3 See for example, Chester Barnard, *The Functions of the Executive* (Cambridge, MA: MIT Press, 1938) and Peter Drucker, *The Practice of Management* (New York: Harper & Row, 1954).
4 F.J. Roethlisberger, *The Elusive Phenomena* (Cambridge, MA: Harvard University Press, 1977).
5 David Brooks, *The Social Animal* (New York: Random House, 2011), x.
6 Dodi Goldman (ed.), *In One's Bones: The Clinical Genius of Winnicott* (Northvale: Jason Aronson, 1993), xi–xii.
7 D.W. Winnicott, "Transitional Objects and Transitional Phenomena," *International Journal of Psychoanalysis*, 34, 1953, 89–97.
8 Robert French and Peter Simpson presented this idea at the 1999 symposium of the International Society for the Psychoanalytic Study of Organizations in Toronto.
9 Edward Shapiro and Wesley Carr, *Lost in Familiar Places* (New Haven: Yale University Press, 1991).
10 While Winnicott focused on the early and primal mother–child relationship, the idea can be extended to fathers, who are much more active parents in the twenty-first century, as well as others who may assume a "parent" role. Bruno Bettelheim extended this line of thinking in his book, *The Good Enough Parent* (New York: Random House, 1987).

11 Shapiro and Carr, *Lost in Familiar Places*, 14.

12 Peter Bregman, "Why Parents Make Great Managers," *Harvard Business Review* blog posting, November 10, 2009. http://blogs.hbr.org/bregman/2009/11/why-parents-make-great-manager.html.

13 Neal Gabler, "The New American Dream," *Boston Globe*, March 31, 2011.

14 See, for example, the work of David McClelland about the achievement motive.

15 Leonard Koren, *Wabi Sabi: for Artists, Designers, Poets and Philosophers* (Berkeley: Stone Bridge Press, 1994).

16 Michael Pollan, *A Place of My Own* (New York: Dell, 1997), 258.

17 David Blum, "Profiles: A Process Larger Than Oneself," *The New Yorker*, May 1, 1989, 46.

18 See www.silkroadproject.org/tabid/144/Default.aspx.

19 Herbie Hancock, Commencement Address, Bentley University, May, 2009.

20 John Lahr, "The Disappearing Act," *The New Yorker*, February 12, 2007, 40.

21 Twyla Tharp (with Mark Reiter), *The Creative Habit* (New York: Simon & Schuster, 2003), 119.

22 Jonah Golberg recently wrote a column about the derivation of the phrase "good enough for government work" in the *National Review* in 2008. There is evidence that the term originally had a positive connotation, meaning that the work met rigorous government standards, although that is the source of some debate. See www.nationalreview.com/corner/164335/good-enough-government-work/jonah-goldberg.

23 The tension between efficiency and creativity, comparing two distinct cultures at 3M was discussed in *Business Week*. See www.businessweek.com/magazine/content/07_24/b4038406.htm.

24 Kathryn Schultz, "The Bright Side of Wrong," *Boston Globe*, June 13, 2010.

25 Kathryn Schultz. See www.boston.com/bostonglobe/ideas/articles/2010/06/13/the_bright_side_of_wrong?mode=PF.

26 Charlene Li, "The Art of Admitting Failure," *Harvard Business Review*, April 6, 2011. http://blogs.hbr.org/cs/2011/03/the_art_of_admitting_failure.html?cm_mmc=email-_-newsletter-_-leadership-_-leadership040611&referral=00206&utm_source=newsletter_leadership&utm_medium=email&utm_campaign=leadership040611.

27 Daniel Pink, *A Whole New Mind* (New York: Riverhead Books, 2005), 25–6.

28 Pink, *A Whole New Mind*, 65–6.

29 John Keats, *The Selected Letters of John Keats* (Garden City: Doubleday Anchor Books, 1956), 103.

30 Anne Morrow Lindbergh, *Gift from the Sea* (New York: Random House, 1955, 1975), 108.

31 Matthew Stewart, *The Management Myth: Why the Experts Keep Getting it Wrong* (New York: Norton, 2009).

32 Alvin Toffler, *Future Shock* (New York: Bantam, 1970).

33 Peter Vaill, *Managing as a Performing Art* (San Francisco: Jossey-Bass, 1989).

34 Howard Gardner, *Frames of Mind* (New York: Basic Books, 1993).

35 Reuven Bar-On, *Bar-On EQi Technical Manual*, 1997.

36 Daniel Goleman, *Emotional Intelligence* (New York: Bantam, 1995).

37 This conceptual debate is nicely captured by Gary Cherniss in "Emotional Intelligence: Toward Clarification of a Concept," *Industrial and Organizational Psychology*, 3(2), 2010, 110–26. The major distinction is between EI as an ability to perceive, use, understand, and manage emotions, and ESC (emotional and social

competencies) that put these abilities into practice and lead to effective or superior performance. The same issue of the journal provides other commentaries related to conceptualization and measurement of emotional intelligence.

38 Daniel Goleman highlights the work of Antonio DiMasio in his second book, *Working with Emotional Intelligence* (New York: Bantam, 1998).

39 See J.L. Bowditch, A.F. Buono, and M.M. Stewart, *A Primer on Organizational Behavior* (Hoboken: John Wiley and Sons, 7th edn, 2007) for a complete survey of leadership theories.

40 Douglas MacGregor, *The Human Side of Enterprise* (New York: McGraw-Hill, 1960).

41 See Harry Levinson, *The Great Jackass Fallacy* (Cambridge, MA: Harvard University Press, 1973) and *Executive* (Cambridge, MA: Harvard University Press, 1978).

42 Ken Blanchard, *Leading at a Higher Level* (Upper Saddle River: Blanchard Management Corporation/Prentice Hall, 2006).

43 Ronald Heifetz, *Leadership Without Easy Answers* (Cambridge, MA: Harvard University Press, 1994).

44 Shapiro and Carr, *Lost in Familiar Places*, 39.

45 Abraham Zaleznik, "Managers and Leaders: Are They Different?" *Harvard Business Review*, May–June, 1977, 73.

46 J. Kotter, "What Leaders Really Do," *Harvard Business Review*, May–June, 1990, 103–11.

47 J. Gosling and H. Mintzberg, "The Five Minds of a Manager," *Harvard Business Review*, November, 2003, 54.

2 Discovering GEMs: A Study of the Best and Worst Managers

1 The survey followed established protocols for data collection and informed consent. The methodology was approved by the University's Institutional Review Board.

2 SPSS Text Analysis for Surveys 3.0 User's Guide (Chicago: SPSS Inc.).

3 Sometimes the root word or theme is used multiple times within one response case or narrative; however, the number of usages recorded is based on the number of cases out of the total in which the word or phrase appears.

4 Marcus Buckingham and Curt Coffman, *First, Break All the Rules* (New York: Simon & Schuster, 1999).

5 Tom Musback, "What Makes a Good Boss?" *San Francisco Chronicle*, May 30, 2010.

6 Daniel Goleman, *Working with Emotional Intelligence* (New York: Bantam, 1998), 40.

7 Anne D. Smith, Donde Ashmos Plowman, and Dennis Duchon, "Everyday Sensegiving: A Closer Look at Successful Plant Managers," *Journal of Applied Behavioral Science*, 46(2), 2010, 220–44.

8 Adam Bryant, "Google's Quest to Build a Better Boss," *New York Times*, March 12, 2011. See www.nytimes.com/2011/03/13/business/13hire.html.

9 Some respondents did not indicate gender in the survey, reducing the total number of responses.

10 Deborah Tannen, *Talking From 9 to 5: Men and Women at Work* (New York: Morrow, 1994).

11 Barry Reece, Rhonda Brandt, and Karen Howie, *Effective Human Relations* (Mason: South-Western Cengage Learning, 2008).

12 Steven Pinker, *The Blank Slate* (New York: Penguin, 2002), 344.

13 Dave Ulrich, Jack Zenger, and Norman Smallwood, *Results-Based Leadership: How Leaders Build the Business and Improve the Bottom Line* (Boston: Harvard Business School Press, 1999), 3.

14 See Daniel Goleman, Richard Boyatsis, and Annie McKee, *Primal Leadership: Realizing the Power of Emotional Intelligence* (Cambridge, MA: Harvard University Press, 2002) and Daniel Goleman, "An EI-Based Theory of Performance," in C. Cherniss, and D. Goleman (eds), *The Emotionally Intelligent Workplace* (San Francisco: Jossey-Bass, 2001), 27–44.

15 Lyle M. Spencer, "The Economic Value of Emotional Intelligence Competencies and EIC-Based HR Programs," in C. Cherniss and D. Goleman (eds), *The Emotionally Intelligent Workplace* (San Francisco: Jossey-Bass, 2001), 45–82.

3 GEMs as Mentors and Teachers

1 The quote is attributed to Allan R. Broadhurst.

2 Harry Levinson, *Executive* (Cambridge, MA: Harvard University Press, 1981).

3 Kathy Kram and Monica Higgins, "A New Approach to Mentoring," *Wall Street Journal*, September 22, 2008.

4 Parker Palmer, *The Courage to Teach* (San Francisco: Jossey-Bass, 1998).

5 D. Winnicott, *The Maturational Processes and the Facilitating Environment* (Madison: International Universities Press, 1965).

6 J.R. Hackman and E.E. Lawler, "Employee Reactions to Job Characteristics," *Journal of Applied Psychology*, 55, 1971, 259–86.

7 Daniel Pink, *Drive: The Surprising Truth about What Motivates Us* (New York: Penguin Group, 2009), 106.

8 Daniel Pink, *Drive*, 107.

9 Drake Bennett, "Out of Line," *Boston Globe*, June 27, 2010, C-1.

10 Edward Shapiro and Wesley Carr, *Lost in Familiar Places* (New Haven: Yale University Press, 1991).

11 http://sports.espn.go.com/nba/news/story?id=1927380.

12 Daniel Katz and Robert Kahn, *The Social Psychology of Organizations* (New York: Wiley, 2nd edn, 1978).

13 James Carroll, "Blurred Boundaries?" *Boston Globe*, May 18, 2009.

14 Virginia Satir, *The New Peoplemaking* (Mountain View: Science and Behavior Books, Inc., 1988).

4 GEMs as Relationship Builders

1 Robert D. Putnam, *Bowling Alone: The Collapse and Revival of American Community* (New York: Simon & Schuster, 2000).

2 Ashley Parker, "And Now, Starring in the West Wing: Ax & Lesser," *New York Times*, June 14, 2009.

3 James Krantz, "The Managerial Couple: Superior-Subordinate Relationships as a Unit of Analysis," in L. Hirshhorn and C. Barnett (eds), *The Psychodynamics of Organizations* (Philadelphia: Temple University Press, 1993), 3.

4 Erik Erikson, *Identity, Youth and Crisis* (New York: Norton, 1968).

5 Manfred Kets de Vries, *The Leadership Mystique* (San Francisco: Jossey-Bass, 2001), 208.

6 Steven Pinker, *The Blank Slate* (New York: Penguin Books, 2002).

7 Roger Fisher and William Ury, *Getting to Yes* (New York: Penguin Books, 1991), 19.

8 Stephen Mitchell, *Relational Concepts in Psychoanalysis* (Cambridge, MA: Harvard University Press, 1988), 5.

9 Laura Crawshaw, *Taming the Abrasive Manager* (San Francisco: Jossey-Bass, 2007).

10 Roman Friedrich, Michael Peterson, and Alex Koster, "The Rise of Generation C," *Strategy and Business*, Booz & Company, Issue 62, Spring, 2011.

11 "Texting is not Talking," *Boston Globe* editorial, June 16, 2009.

12 Malcolm Gladwell, "Small Change: Why the Revolution will not be Tweeted," *The New Yorker*, October 4, 2010, 42–9.

13 Steven McCornack, *Reflect and Relate* (Boston: Bedford/St. Martin's, 2nd edn, 2010), 222.

14 D. Winnicott, "The Capacity to be Alone," *International Journal of Psychoanalysis*, 39(5), 1958, 416–20.

15 The same phrase was coincidentally used as a caption in the letters section of *The New York Times Magazine*, August 29, 2010, 8.

16 See George Carlin, *When Will Jesus Bring the Pork Chops?* (New York: Hyperion, 2004).

17 The name given in the response has been removed to preserve anonymity.

18 Dan Beuttner was interviewed on National Public Radio, *Weekend Edition Sunday*, November 28, 2010. See www.npr.org/2010/11/24/131571885/how-to-thrive-dan-buettner-s-secrets-of-happiness?sc=emaf.

5 GEMs as Models of Integrity

1 Warren Bennis and Burt Nanus, *Leaders: Strategies for Taking Charge* (New York: HarperCollins, 1985), 20.

2 Aaron Nurick, "Teacher and Therapist: An Integration of Educator Roles," *Organizational Behavior Teaching Review*, 12(3), 1987–8, 91.

3 Malcolm Gladwell, "Cocksure," *The New Yorker*, July 27, 2009, 24–8.

4 Gladwell, "Cocksure," 28.

5 David Callahan, *The Cheating Culture* (Orlando: Harcourt, Inc., 2002).

6 Irving Janis, *Victims of Groupthink* (Boston: Houghton Mifflin, 1972).

7 William H. Peace, "The Hard Work of Being a Soft Manager," *Harvard Business Review*, November–December, 1991, 40–7.

8 Peace, "The Hard Work," 41.

9 Peace, "The Hard Work," 40.

10 The story originally included names that have been edited out to preserve anonymity.

11 Joseph W. Weiss, *Business Ethics: A Stakeholder and Issues Management Approach* (Mason: Cengage Learning/South-Western, 5th edn, 2009).

12 David Brooks, *The Social Animal* (New York: Random House, 2011), 285.

13 Pinker elaborates on the work of Jonathan Haidt in his article, "The Moral Instinct," *The New York Times Magazine*, January 13, 2008.

14 Rushworth Kidder, *Moral Courage* (New York: HarperCollins, 2005).

15 See for example, Stephen Covey, *Principle-Centered Leadership* (New York: Fireside, 1990).

16 L. Stapley, *Individuals, Groups and Organizations Beneath the Surface* (London: Karnac, 2006), 60–1.

17 R. Lubit, "The Long-Term Organizational Impact of Destructively Narcissistic Managers," *Academy of Management Executive*, 16(1), 2002, 127–38.
18 J. Bowditch, A. Buono, and M. Stewart, *A Primer on Organizational Behavior* (Hoboken: John Wiley and Sons, 7th edn, 2007), 239.
19 Lawrence Gould, "Contemporary Perspectives on Personal and Organizational Authority: The Self in a System of Work Relationships," in L. Hirschhorn and C. Barnett (eds), *The Psychodynamics of Organizations* (Philadelphia: Temple University Press, 1993).
20 Thomas Teal, "The Human Side of Management," *Harvard Business Review*, November–December, 1996, 37.

6 Becoming a GEM

1 These ideas were referenced in a keynote speech by Ben Cameron, Program Director of Arts for the Doris Duke Charitable Foundation, at the League of American Orchestras National Conference, June, 2010.
2 The concept of generativity comes from Erik Erikson, *Identity: Youth and Crisis* (New York: Norton, 1968), 138–9.
3 Dave Ulrich, Norm Smallwood, and Kate Sweetman, *The Leadership Code: Five Rules to Lead By* (Boston: Harvard Business Press, 2009).
4 M. Allison Buck, "Mentoring: A Promising Strategy for Creating and Sustaining a Learning Organization," *Adult Learning*, 15(3–4), 2004, 8–11.
5 Michael Watkins, *Harvard Business Review* blog posting, http://blogs.hbr.org/watkins/2007/10/infectious_leadership.html?cm_mmc=npv-_-listserv-_-OCT_2007-_-LeadershipShortTest.
6 Thomas Teal, "The Human Side of Management," *Harvard Business Review*, November–December, 1996, 35–44.
7 Daniel Goleman, Richard Boyatsis, and Annie McKee, *Primal Leadership* (Boston: Harvard Business School Publishing, 2002), 5.
8 Christopher Bollas, *The Shadow of the Object* (New York: Columbia University Press, 1987).
9 Robert French and Peter Simpson, "Our Best Work Happens When We Don't Know What We're Doing," presented at the International Society for the Psychoanalytic Study of Organizations annual symposium, 1999, Toronto.
10 Ken Bain, *What the Best College Teachers Do* (Cambridge, MA: Harvard University Press, 2004), 145.
11 Anthony Athos, "Contingencies Beyond Reasoning," *Exchange: The Organizational Behavior Teaching Journal*, 4(2), 1979, 9.
12 Anthony Athos, "Contingencies Beyond Reasoning," 12.
13 Donald Schon, *The Reflective Practitioner* (New York: Basic Books, 1983) and Edward Shapiro and Wesley Carr, *Lost in Familiar Places* (New Haven: Yale University Press, 1991).
14 Ronald Heifetz and Marty Linsky, *Leadership on the Line* (Boston: Harvard Business School Press, 2002).
15 See Joan Peyser, *Bernstein: A Biography* (New York: Beech Tree Books, William Morrow, 1987).
16 These observations are from personal experience, informal conversations with musicians, and the perspective of critics such as Jeremy Eichler, "The Opening Movement: After Five Seasons it's Levine's BSO: Calmed Down and Charged Up," *Boston Globe*, February 22, 2009.

17 These ideas were presented by Mr. Morlot at an informal talk at Tanglewood, the summer home of the Boston Symphony, on August 19, 2010.

18 Jessica Shambora, "Advice from a Maestro," *Fortune*, April 11, 2011, 37–9.

19 A.D. Smith, D.A. Plowman, and D. Duchon, "Everyday Sensegiving: A Closer Look at Successful Plant Managers," *Journal of Applied Behavioral Science*, 46(2), 2010, 220–44.

20 See Steven J. Stein and Howard E. Book, *The EQ Edge* (Toronto: Stoddart, 2000) and David R. Caruso and Peter Salovey, *The Emotionally Intelligent Manager* (San Francisco: Jossey-Bass, 2004) for a full discussion of the multiple dimensions of emotional intelligence along with helpful exercises.

21 Harry Levinson, *Ready, Fire, Aim: Avoiding Management by Impulse* (Cambridge, MA: The Levinson Institute, 1986).

22 Peter Simpson, Robert French, and Charles E. Harvey, "Leadership and Negative Capability," *Human Relations*, 55(10), 2002, 1209–26.

23 Alex Koppelman, "Sotomayor: The Triumph of Empathy," *Salon*, May 26, 2009.

24 Joseph Thai, "John Paul Stevens," in D.S. Tanenhaus (ed.), *The Encyclopedia of the Supreme Court of the United States* (New York: Macmillan, 2008).

25 Stein and Book, *The EQ Edge*, 113.

26 Alfred Margulies, *The Empathic Imagination* (New York: Norton, 1989), 3.

27 This wonderful analogy was presented by Daniel Pink in *Drive* (New York: Riverhead Books, 2009), 91.

28 Lawrence Gould, "Contemporary Perspectives on Personal and Organizational Authority: The Self in a System of Work Relationships," in L. Hirschhorn and C. Barnett (eds), *The Psychodynamics of Organizations* (Philadelphia: Temple University Press, 1993), 50.

29 Simpson *et al.*, "Leadership and Negative Capability."

30 D.W. Winnicott, *Playing and Reality* (London and New York: Routledge, 1990).

31 T. Peters and R. Waterman, *In Search of Excellence* (New York: Harper & Row, 1982), 122.

32 Information for this process was provided by Jim Knight, Senior Director of Training and Development, Hard Rock International.

33 Dean Smith, Gerald Bell, and John Kilgo, *The Carolina Way: Leadership Lessons from a Life in Coaching* (New York: Penguin), 2004.

34 Steven Covey, *The Seven Habits of Highly Effective People* (New York: Free Press, 1989).

35 This phrase was gleaned from an interactive concert for young people by conductor Thomas Wilkins with the Boston Symphony Orchestra.

36 See National Geographic facts about wildfires at http://environment.nationalgeographic.com/environment/natural-disasters/wildfires/.

37 Stephen Covey uses a similar metaphor of the emotional bank account in his *Seven Habits*.

38 Robert Bolton, *People Skills* (New York: Simon & Schuster, 1979, 1986).

39 The "so that" idea comes from Dave Ulrich *et al.*, *Results Based Leadership* cited in Chapter 2. Dave Ulrich, Jack Zenger, and Norman Smallwood, *Results-Based Leadership: How Leaders Build the Business and Improve the Bottom Line* (Boston: Harvard Business School Press, 1999), 3.

40 See www.marshallmcluhan.com.

41 Daniel Pink, *A Whole New Mind* (New York: Riverhead, 2005), 20.

42 Richard Kilburg and Richard Diedrich (eds), *The Wisdom of Coaching: Essential*

Papers in Consulting Psychology for a World of Change (Washington, D.C.: American Psychological Association, 2007).

43 A. Nurick, "Consulting and EQ: Enhancing Emotional Intelligence in the Workplace," in A. Buono, *Current Trends in Management Consulting* (Greenwich, CT: Information Age Publishing, 2001), 71–86.

44 Drake Bennett, "Executive Honor: Can an 'MBA Oath' Fix What's Wrong with Business?" *Boston Globe*, May 16, 2010.

45 Paul Bloom, "The Moral Life of Babies," *The New York Times Magazine*, May 3, 2010.

46 Paul Clemens, "Nearly Perfect in Detroit," *New York Times*, June 4, 2010.

47 K. Lewin, *Principles of Topological Psychology* (New York: McGraw-Hill, 1936).

48 Elliot Aronson, *The Social Animal* (New York: Worth, 10th edn, 2008).

49 Harry Levinson, *Executive* (Cambridge, MA: Harvard University Press, 1981), 19.

50 Anthony Athos and John Gabarro, *Interpersonal Behavior in Management* (Englewood Cliffs: Prentice Hall, 1978).

51 Robin J. Ely, Debra E. Meyerson, and Martin N. Davidson, "Rethinking Political Correctness," *Harvard Business Review*, September, 2006, 80.

52 Ely *et al.*, "Rethinking Political Correctness," 80.

53 For a full appreciation of ethics applied to business, see Joseph W. Weiss, *Business Ethics: A Stakeholder and Issues Management Approach* (Mason: Cengage Learning/South-Western, 5th edn, 2009).

54 Bentley University Center for Business Ethics.

55 Aronson, *The Social Animal*, 251.

56 Stein and Book, *The EQ Edge*, 125.

57 These questions are adapted from Stein and Book, *The EQ Edge*, 133.

58 Rajendra Sisodia, David Wolfe, and Jagdith Sheth, *Firms of Endearment: The Pursuit of Purpose and Profit* (Upper Saddle River: Wharton School Publishing, 2007).

59 "Starbucks Hits 40 Feeling Perky," *USA Today*, March 7, 2011, 1B.

60 See http://about.zappos.com/our-unique-culture/zappos-core-values and www.deliveringhappinessbook.com/.

61 Gould, "Contemporary Perspectives on Personal and Organizational Authority," 62.

Index

Page numbers in *italics* denote tables, those in **bold** denote figures.